FROM THE KITCHEN OF

&

....

Just Married

Just Married

A COOKBOOK FOR NEWLYWEDS

Caroline Chambers

PHOTOGRAPHS BY
LINDA PUGLIESE

CHRONICLE BOOKS
SAN FRANCISCO

Library of Congress Cataloging-in-Publication Data

Names: Chambers, Caroline, author.

Title: Just married / by Caroline Chambers.

Description: San Francisco, California : Chronicle books, [2018] | Includes index.

Identifiers: LCCN 2017049256 | ISBN 9781452166711 (hardcover : alk. paper)

Subjects: LCSH: Cooking for two. | LCGFT: Cookbooks.

Classification: LCC TX714 .C64195 2018 | DDC 641.5/612—dc23 LC record available
    at https://lccn.loc.gov/2017049256

Manufactured in China

Photography by Linda Pugliese

Food styling by Mariana Velasquez

Prop styling by Jeanne Lurvey

Designed by Anne Kenady

Typesetting by DC Typography

10 9 8 7 6 5 4 3 2 1

Chronicle books and gifts are available at special quantity discounts to corporations, professional associations, literacy programs, and other organizations. For details and discount information, please contact our premiums department at corporatesales@ chroniclebooks.com or at 1-800-759-0190.

Chronicle Books LLC
680 Second Street
San Francisco, California 94107
www.chroniclebooks.com

To George, my sous chef for life

Contents

"Just married" is a delicious stage of life: one to be savored, and nurtured, and nourished to grow strong. With the memories of the actual wedding behind you, now is the time to begin your new life together, creating more memories. If you're anything like me, your most special memories usually involve food . . . sometimes just the smells of something familiar can transport you back to those times. Maybe you served something special at your reception because of its special significance to you as a couple. Maybe you first cooked a childhood favorite for your love as a gift. Perhaps a favorite relative slipped a guarded old family recipe scribbled on a worn notecard into your wedding gift.

Coming together at the end, or beginning, of the day to share—thoughts, feelings, hopes, and dreams—over a meal can be a very intimate and enriching experience. But who has time to cook? Problem solved . . . with the easy, delicious, and memory-making meals included here.

I realize that, more than ever, busy couples share the sometimes joyous, often burdensome, task of putting a meal on the table, as long gone are the days of doting housewives slaving over Julia Child's Beef Bourguignon for 7-plus hours. Often the first person home from work is on dinner duty—regardless of who holds the title of best cook in the marriage. Maybe both of you cook; maybe neither of you cooks. *Just Married* is here to help.

I've created this book for both the couples who see Thai takeout on the couch in front of an episode of the latest HBO hit as a success, and for those couples who want to expand their culinary achievements. This collection of recipes meets every newlywed's requirements—quick breakfasts for busy workday mornings, slow recipes for sweet, lazy Sundays, quick and healthy salads and bowls, healthy and decadent soups and salads, dinners that take fewer than 30 minutes, more elaborate dinners for special nights at home together, inexpensive meals to entertain a crowd, and, of course, a few (sweet) surprises.

Demanding work hours, busy social calendars, and the pursuit of hobbies mean newlyweds often eat breakfast on the go and dinners in a hanger (hunger + anger) -infused hurry. Don't let this describe you.

My own newlywed story provides the backdrop for this cookbook. From the moment we locked eyes at a hog roast on a North Carolina farm, my relationship with my now-husband, George, has revolved around food. Our first dates consisted of lengthy drives to find the best Chinese food in the state as well as coaxing a Trader Joe's-assisted feast from old hand-me-down pots and pans.

For our one-year dating anniversary, George saved up to take me to Lantern, in Chapel Hill, North Carolina, a beautiful restaurant that would achieve a James Beard Award years later. Now, when planning vacations, our itineraries are meticulously planned around where to eat—the best banh mi in Vietnam, the most authentic haggis in Scotland, or the freshest fish tacos in Mexico.

For the first (many) years of our relationship, I was the family cook (it was only natural; I owned a catering business). When I sold my catering company to work full-time in culinary consulting in San Francisco, the new schedule rocked our (eating) world. In one of my first weeks back to a full-time office gig, I returned home around 8 p.m., exhausted from a day on my feet in the test kitchen. After kissing me hello, George asked, "What's for dinner?" I almost hit him on the back of the head with the skillet that he *should* have been using to cook me dinner!

Instead, I put the skillet down and cooked us a delicious meal—explaining my every move to George, who had just received a major dressing down and was obediently scribbling cooking notes. George, for the first time in his life, was confronted with the task of occasionally grocery shopping and cooking for two. It became our ritual that, every day, as soon as I began my hour-long commute home, I'd call to instruct him on how to start dinner. By the time I got home, the vegetables would be halfway through their roast, the chicken resting in a simple marinade, and whatever back-of-the-fridge ingredients could go into a salad would be gathered on the counter.

Even if I arrived home very late and George had already eaten, he always paused his own work to sit with me while I ate, and we talked about our days. We were coping with a move to a new city, a new and tiny apartment, new jobs, and new friends. This small shift in our cooking responsibilities and our dedication to eating dinner together helped us forge through an emotional and tricky transition.

Young couples undergo many changes in their first few years of marriage: buying their first house, changing jobs, moving to new cities, making new "couple friends," even growing their new family with children. But one thing has remained constant, no matter what (or where) the dinner table is—be it outdoors where we ate year-round in Coronado, California, because a table didn't fit inside our 400-square-foot [37-sq-m] house; the beautiful oak table in the Peaks Resort lobby where we ate microwave-prepared meals during our summer in Telluride, Colorado; the furnished-student-housing table in our Stanford apartment; or the rickety old table with an old church pew for half its seating in our rundown Tribeca loft—that is the place where our young marriage flourished. Table or no table, hodgepodge or gourmet meal, families truly come together here.

So my gift to you is this cookbook—all those notes and instructions to George about dinner and the results of years of trial and error in the catering business and recipe development world, compiled here, to make your precious moments around the table easy, delicious, and stress-free.

Wedding Registry

My guide to the perfect wedding registry is divided into three sections:

- "Vital Tools" are compulsory for easy, stress-free cooking for two.
- "Nice-to-Have Tools" include tools that help you cook for a crowd and in ways that are not particularly necessary, but add pizazz to your cooking repertoire (an outdoor grill, for instance).
- "Fun-to-Have Tools" include tools so completely unnecessary you'll probably only use them a few times a year. But, when you do use them, you'll be glad you have them.

VITAL TOOLS

COFFEE MAKER Our coffee maker is, by far, our most utilized kitchen tool. Do your research, and buy one that meets your needs. We swear by our Technivorm Moccamaster.

8-IN [20-CM] NONSTICK OVENPROOF SKILLET ideal size for small meals for one or two people, and for making omelets.

10-IN [25-CM] CAST IRON SKILLET My cast iron skillet is my most beloved kitchen tool. Follow your manufacturer's instructions for cleaning and seasoning it—take care of it, and it will take care of you. Wonderful for baking, searing meats, homemade pizza, frittatas, and so much more.

12-IN [30.5-CM] NONSTICK SKILLET perfect for stir-fries, sautéing greens, cooking for a crowd.

DUTCH OVENS IN MULTIPLE SIZES If you find yourself using a Dutch oven frequently, it's nice to have multiple sizes for different needs. I prefer a 2-qt [2-L] size for cooking for two. I use my 3-qt [2.8-L] Dutch oven to make baked egg dishes, Garlic Confit and Thyme, Dutch Oven Bread (page 132), Red Curry Mussels (page 150), and so much more; a 9-qt [8.5-L] size is good for cooking large quantities (I use mine to make massive batches of chili); a 5½-qt [5-L] size is the perfect compromise if you simply don't need multiple Dutch ovens. Select one that is circular instead of oval for the most even cooking.

Y VEGETABLE PEELER Buy inexpensive vegetable peelers and replace them every few months, as they grow dull.

INSTANT-READ THERMOMETER A good instant-read meat thermometer is *so* important for cooking meat correctly every time!

FISH SPATULA I use my stainless steel fish spatula for *everything*. It's flexible but sturdy and perfect for flipping pancakes, fried eggs, or, yes, fish.

WOODEN SPOON One good wooden spoon is all you need for making soups or sauces. Wood doesn't absorb heat like stainless steel, so it's the ideal tool to avoid burning your mouth as you taste (and stir) along the way.

HEAT-RESISTANT SILICONE SPATULAS My favorite tool for sautéing.

MICROPLANE GRATER for zesting citrus and shaving cheese or chocolate over dishes.

BOX GRATER I like a box grater with several hole sizes. Use it to shred vegetables and cheese.

METAL BOWLS I like to have two large metal bowls, two medium metal bowls, and two small metal bowls for mixing, marinating, sauce making, and any other needs.

CUTTING BOARD Use inexpensive plastic cutting boards for meats; use an attractive wooden board you can leave out on your counter all the time for cutting bread, produce, etc. I also like to serve right from my wooden board, using it as a large platter.

CHEF'S KNIFE A really good 8-in [20-cm] chef's knife will handle most of your cutting needs. I highly suggest going to a kitchen store and "trying out" different knives before making your decision. Each knife brand has a different style and feel.

PARING KNIFE A 3-in [7.5-cm] paring knife is the best tool for more delicate cutting jobs like stemming straw-berries, deveining shrimp, or segmenting citrus.

LONG SERRATED KNIFE A 9-in [23-cm] or longer serrated knife will do the trick when it comes to slicing through items with a hard outside and tender inside, such as a crusty loaf of bread or a large piece of seared meat.

RIMMED BAKING SHEETS Two or three baking sheets are all you need to fulfill most of your roasting and baking needs. Be sure to check your oven size before purchasing: A standard oven will fit a half sheet pan, but our first two houses had smaller ovens that only fit quarter sheet pans!

MUFFIN TIN for muffins and personal frittatas (page 42)

TART PAN WITH A REMOVABLE BOTTOM Removable bottoms eliminate the trickiness of releasing tarts and pies from the pan.

HIGH-POWERED BLENDER Vitamix is my preferred brand and the preferred brand of many top chefs and restaurants. They are quite expensive but completely worth it. I make soups, sauces, and smoothies in my Vitamix.

STAND MIXER My KitchenAid stand mixer has a per-manent spot on my kitchen counter; it's crucial for mixing bread and cookie doughs. But a handheld mixer will do.

COLANDER STRAINER for draining pasta, or washing vegetables; if metal, it can also be snuggled into a large pot and used as a steamer basket in a pinch.

NICE-TO-HAVE TOOLS

12-IN [30.5-CM] CAST IRON SKILLET A 10-in [25-cm] cast iron skillet is great for cooking for two, but a larger skillet lets you cook larger quantities.

FOOD PROCESSOR [7-QT/6.6-L] You'll use this for shredding cheese, chopping vegetables, making piecrusts, and so many other things! I put this in the "nice to have" section because you can achieve most of the same things using a high-powered blender or by hand.

MINI FOOD PROCESSOR When cooking for two, it's nice to have a mini food processor for small portions.

OUTDOOR GRILL Having an outdoor grill will hugely expand your cooking repertoire. Of course, you need an outdoor space to have an outdoor grill, a feat that can prove rather tricky for city-dwelling newlyweds.

SILPAT (SILICONE) BAKING MATS These wash-able mats turn your baking sheets into nonstick surfaces. They also make cleanup a breeze.

BONING KNIFE The long, flexible blade of a boning knife is perfect for butchering delicate cuts of meat, especially removing fat or skin from meat.

GRILL PAN A grill pan is an awesome, but completely unnecessary, tool. It basically provides the same utility of a cast iron skillet, but the ridges on the pan give what-ever you're cooking the illusion of charred grill marks. I love mine, because it really does make food look beauti-ful, but if you're short on space, it's redundant.

ROLLING PIN If you plan to make a classic pie or my Rustic Cherry Pistachio Galette (page 252), you need a rolling pin. In a pinch, you can use a wine bottle.

STEAMER I love my adjustable steamer insert. Insert this tool into any pot that you already own to steam vegetables or a filet of fish with no oil for an ultimate detox meal.

COCKTAIL SHAKER A good cocktail takes a dinner party to the next level.

FUN-TO-HAVE TOOLS

ICE CREAM MAKER Making fresh ice cream at home is such a treat.

SPIRALIZER Entirely unnecessary, but a fun tool to introduce into your kitchen. Zucchini noodles are all the rage, but you can also use a spiralizer to quickly prepare thinly sliced onions for pickling, carrots for salads, or potatoes for curly fries.

FONDUE POT Fondue pots are so much fun for a party—who doesn't love dunking bread into a pot full of melty hot cheese! Set it out as an appetizer for a large party, or place it in the middle of the table and make it the main course for a smaller dinner party.

TABLE DÉCOR Choose flower vases, linen napkins, napkin rings, and placemats that express your personal style. I love using linen napkins when it's just the two of us on a Tuesday night; they make even the simplest meal feel special.

WAFFLE IRON You might only use it five or six times a year, but *man*, will your family be happy when you do. As a bonus, you can use it to make waffle-y paninis!

Stocked

My siblings and I grew up in awe of the way our mother could turn a seemingly empty refrigerator into a delicious, wholesome meal for five. She kept a well-stocked pantry and was such a confident cook that she always managed to pull off mealtime seamlessly, even when she was too busy with three children and a full-time advertising career to make it to the grocery store. She'd whip her way around the kitchen, making the most colossal mess and, 30 minutes later, spaghetti carbonara, taco pie, tuna casserole, pasta bolognese, or one of her other specialties would hit the dinner table.

Luckily, cooking from a well-stocked pantry (which I consider my dry storage, freezer, and refrigerator [for long-lasting items]) is a skill I inherited from my mother. By stocking up on a few staples (canned tomatoes and beans, dry grains, frozen meats, for example) several times a year, it's always easy to pull together a nourishing meal in a pinch without a trip to the grocery store.

There are a few things that we always buy organic (see page 21), but, for others, we just opt for the least expensive product available. We are on a newlywed budget, after all!

PANTRY

CANNED TOMATOES High-quality, whole, peeled canned tomatoes are in heavy rotation at our house. Eggs are poached in flavorful tomato sauces, a whole can gets thrown into a pot of chili. A few recipes in this book call for canned diced tomatoes, but I mostly just buy whole and chop them, if needed.

CANNED BEANS (black, cannellini, kidney) I always have a few cans of beans in the pantry. Drain and simmer in chicken stock with fresh herbs for the simplest side dish, or throw them straight from the can into salads for a vegetarian protein kick.

TOMATO PASTE For depth and flavor, add this ingredient to soups, sauces, curries, and the like. For storage reasons, I prefer to buy tomato paste in a tube, but if you can find only canned tomato paste, shape any leftovers into a thin plastic-wrapped log, freeze, and simply slice off a bit whenever you need it.

CANNED TUNA The ultimate pantry protein. A little mayo, some chopped celery, a handful of raisins, and a sprinkle of curry powder are all you need for the most delicious tuna salad.

VINEGAR Acid is one of the fundamental components of a well-balanced dish, and I often rely on vinegars to provide it. I use white wine vinegar when I need something mild, usually for salad dressings. Rice vinegar is key to cooking Asian cuisine, but I use it for dressings and cooking, too. Sherry vinegar is sharp; I use it when there's a good deal of fat in the dish. Apple cider vinegar is my go-to, whether to add acidity to a rich meat dish (Fig-Glazed Pork Belly, page 183) or to whisk with mustard, maple syrup, and good extra-virgin olive oil for my favorite dressing. Red wine vinegar adds a mildly fruity, sharp flavor boost.

OIL Grapeseed oil and olive oil for cooking at high temperatures. Extra-virgin olive oil should never be heated, just drizzled in its raw form. Sesame oil adds a rich, nutty flavor to dishes and should, generally, be used raw but can be added to food that's near the end of cooking.

ASSORTED PASTAS I love cooking with new shapes and flavors but always keep spaghetti, bow tie, and rotini pastas on hand.

QUINOA America's favorite grain has a permanent spot on my shelves. It's nutritious and can be used in so many different ways. I crisp it up like a healthy crouton to make my Garlicky Quinoa Crispies (page 87), and I use it as a base for heartier, nutritious dishes such as Harissa Braised Short Ribs (page 205) in place of mashed potatoes or rice. If it's not indicated as pre-rinsed on the package, always rinse it before cooking to remove its natural bitter (saponin) coating.

RICE I use white rice, brown rice, and wild black rice interchangeably, depending on my mood. White rice is the most comforting and familiar, brown rice is a more nutritious, nuttier-tasting alternative, and wild rice is tougher to the bite, more complex. You'll find recipes for a variety in these pages, but feel free to use your favorite or whatever you have on hand.

ALMOND BUTTER Add this tasty ingredient to your granola and yogurt for a protein boost, use it in Coronado Cookies (page 240), or make my spicy and addictive Sriracha Almond Butter Sauce (page 234) with it.

CHIA SEEDS This powerful superfood is packed with omegas-3s, protein, vitamins, and minerals. Use them to boost your smoothie's nutrition, make Raspberry-Coconut Chia Pudding (page 36), stir 2 Tbsp into your favorite granola recipe (page 27), or use as a thickener instead of cornstarch or flour, as in the Strawberry Rose Chia Jam (page 34). If you need a vegan substitute for eggs as a thickener in baking, try a chia egg: For each egg needed, mix 1 tablespoon chia seeds with 3 tablespoons boiling water. Let sit for 5 minutes, and add to your recipe in place of the eggs.

OATS Old-fashioned rolled oats can be tossed into cookies, made into overnight oats, or simply eaten as oatmeal for a nutritious, fibrous breakfast.

REFRIGERATOR

MAYONNAISE Creamy vinaigrettes, delicious sandwich spreads (mayonnaise + a smidge of red curry paste + fresh lime juice is my secret sauce), deviled eggs, and my Grilled Corn and Tahini Salad (page 224) all feature mayo. Many days, lunch is a slice of toasted leftover bread swiped with mayonnaise and topped with whatever cheese and meat I can find.

MUSTARD I keep Dijon and whole-grain mustards on hand to make zippy dressings and kicked-up sauces. A little mustard goes a long way.

GOCHUJANG This funky, sweet, and spicy Korean chile paste adds incredible complexity to dishes. Use it in moderation, as some brands can be seriously spicy. Stir it into ketchup, use it in a marinade (as in Korean Sliced Beef, page 182), or try it in place of harissa in Harissa Braised Short Ribs (page 205).

SAMBAL OELEK Sambal oelek provides more direct, acidic heat than gochujang. Stir sambal with a bit of sesame oil and sugar for a simple sauce, or use it in the Crispy Brussels Sprouts with Spicy Orange Sauce (page 228) or Tangy Vietnamese Dressing (page 84).

SRIRACHA Sriracha is mildly spicy, perfectly acidic, and super flavorful. It can be used in place of sambal oelek or gochujang in a real pinch; just use a bit more than the recipe calls for because it's much milder.

CURRY PASTE I have a refrigerator full of every curry paste available on the U.S. market, but yellow and red are my favorites. You can use them interchangeably, though heat levels vary by brand and by color. Try stirring a bit of paste into soups or sauces for a complex heat, like in my Red Curry Mussels (page 150).

MISO PASTE Miso paste is a fermented soybean paste that adds a punchy, salty, umami flavor to dressings, sauces, soups, and anything else you might like. I like white miso, which has a milder flavor than red miso.

TAHINI Tahini is a staple in Middle Eastern kitchens. It is a paste created from ground sesame seeds, with a nutty taste that adds richness and depth to any dish.

EGGS Eggs are my all-time favorite ingredient. Use them to make rich, silky sauces, or cook them in any number of ways (see page 47). Add a boiled or poached egg to a salad or veggie side to instantly make it an entrée.

FRESH HERBS I always have fresh herbs on hand, whether they're fresh from my garden or stashed in my refrigerator. A large bunch of fresh parsley or cilantro typically costs 99 cents and will stay fresh for 5 to 7 days when wrapped in a damp paper towel and stored in a resealable plastic bag. Perhaps even more than for their taste, I use fresh herbs to instantly beautify any plate of food. Leftover meatballs microwaved on a plate? A smattering of fresh Parmesan, chopped fresh parsley, and red pepper flakes make them instantly look restaurant quality.

EDIBLE FLOWERS Most edible flowers add little in terms of taste, but they *will* make you look like a pro. I like plucking the petals and scattering them over salads or veggie sides. If you have an herb garden, it's worth planting a few varieties of edible flowers (I like carnations and chrysanthemums), because even just a few petals go a long way.

FREEZER

PEAS Toss them into salads, soups, or braises at the last minute. Mix with store-bought pesto, shaved Parmesan, and toasted walnuts for the easiest, most delicious side. Toss into curries, soups, and stir-fries at the last minute so they defrost but retain their crispness.

CHOPPED SPINACH When I need a boost of greens, I toss a bit of frozen spinach into my morning smoothie. For a quick side dish, sauté frozen spinach with a bit of chicken broth and lemon juice.

SHRIMP I buy sustainable, peeled, deveined frozen shrimp in bulk bags to keep around for speedy dinners like Coconut Milk Shrimp (page 151) or Shrimp Fajita Salad with Avocado Cilantro Dressing (page 92).

ASSORTED FRUITS FOR SMOOTHIES I buy big bags of frozen fruits for smoothies or baking, but I also keep a big resealable plastic freezer bag in the freezer to freeze fresh fruit on its last leg for later use.

ALWAYS ORGANIC

MEAT I know, I know, organic meat is expensive. But you can still put meat on the table as often as you like by decreasing portion sizes and increasing healthy, filling accompaniments such as grains and sides. Flank steak, chicken thighs, and pork shoulder get the most play at my house.

LETTUCE Nonorganic leafy greens and fresh spinach are hotbeds for pesticides, so I always go organic with greens. I like to keep romaine lettuce heads and fresh spinach on hand at all times for quick salads or sautés. Arugula, Little Gem lettuce, and kale are also in heavy rotation.

CITRUS If using the citrus peel in a recipe, it's important to buy organic, since the absorbent peel can contain a lot of pesticides and other chemicals. I keep fresh lemons on hand at all times for a hit of bright acidity in dishes.

FRUIT When I can afford to do so, I buy my thin-skinned fruit (berries, apples, pears, etc.) organic. I like to keep whatever's seasonal on hand for breakfast, tossing in salads, or even cooking in savory dishes such as Crispy Chicken Thighs with Shallots and Nectarines (page 174).

How to Use This Book

When cooking from a recipe, the single most important ingredient for success is to *read the entire recipe* before starting to cook it. Why? You might realize you don't have the right kind of skillet, and need to improvise from the get-go. You might realize you don't actually need to buy a whole bag of cornmeal because the directions indicate you can substitute flour. It will save you time, money, and a whole lot of frustration.

Reading the entire recipe first is especially important when cooking from this book because so much important information is provided in the notes. This book has nine categories of notes, all of which are designed to make you a better cook and to help make cooking the stress-free, joyous occasion it should be. Here's how:

LEFTOVERS ARE A GOOD THING

All recipes in this book (except chapter 8, "Feasts with Friends") are written to happily satisfy two eaters. If a recipe's serving size is for more than two, this label indicates the recipe will be delicious served as leftovers. Red Snapper with Leeks and Cherry Tomatoes (page 172) is written for two to eat immediately, because leftover fish is kind of a bummer. Grilled Corn and Tahini Salad (page 224), on the other hand, is written for four because it's absolutely delicious the next day, and you should pack it for lunch at the office. Check the "Leftovers are a Good Thing" notes for ideas on how to repurpose leftover ingredients and dishes.

MAKE AHEAD

The "make-ahead" annotations instruct you on what recipe elements you can prep ahead of time to make mealtime quicker and easier.

SEASONALITY

The "Seasonality" tips teach you how to make substitutions based on the season. For instance, it's always better to use frozen corn when fresh isn't in season!

TOOL TIP

Every now and then, a specific tool is required to best execute a dish. In the "Tool Tip" section, I talk about other ways to use that newly acquired tool, or I give an option for how best to execute the technique without the tool.

SPECIAL INGREDIENT

So many of my newlywed friends have the same complaint when I ask about their cooking habits: "Every time I make a recipe, I end up spending more than $60 because I have to buy some special ingredient that I'll never use again. It's cheaper just to order take-out." The "Special Ingredient" notation provides at least three alternate uses for any ingredient deemed "out of the ordinary" to help you get your money's worth from every ingredient you purchase. For instance, try stirring harissa into your scrambled eggs, mixing it with mayo for a spicy sandwich condiment, and dressing up plain store-bought hummus by swirling in 1 Tbsp.

DO YOUR THING

The "Do Your Thing" section provides ingredient substitutions, alternate flavor combinations, and fun tips for how to adapt the recipe to suit your tastes.

MAKE IT A MEAL

Some dishes, such as Chipotle Carnitas Tacos (page 206) are a meal in themselves, while others, such as Grilled Flank Steak with Charred Poblano Romesco (Page 202) would do better with a side. Look for "Make It a Meal" tips for my suggestions on what to pair together, or how to alter a recipe easily to make it a complete meal, like adding an extra cup [20 g] of arugula and topping with grilled chicken.

COOKING SCHOOL

"Cooking School" tips are designed to help you become a better cook. Cooking techniques and knife skills used in the recipes are highlighted here to help you learn and use them in the future.

BUY SMART

Here you'll find clues for how to get the best deal, how to take advantage of the butcher's knife skills so there's less work to do at home, and how to repurpose whatever you have in your fridge so you don't have to buy anything at all.

You'll also find a few "Back Pocket Recipes" throughout the book, which are simple add-ons to make your dishes a little more interesting. They can usually be thrown together from items you already have in your pantry.

Breakfast

ON THE FLY

We all know breakfast is the most important meal of the day, but how many of us actually treat it that way? More often, weekday breakfasts are treated as an afterthought—a protein bar snagged at a convenience store, a secretly sugary parfait from Starbucks coffee shop, or, worst of all, nothing.

I've found that with a bit of planning (Hazelnut-Maple Granola, facing page), and an arsenal of quickie recipes (Almond-Banana Smoothie, page 28) in my back pocket, a nourishing, balanced, fueling workday breakfast isn't out of reach. All recipes in this chapter can either be made in 15 minutes or fewer, or prepped and reheated as you run out the door to start your busy day—and since this book is about cooking for two, you'll get yourself and your special someone off to a healthy, well-fueled start.

Hazelnut-Maple Granola

George and I spent our newlywed years moving from one tiny, one-bedroom home to another, but we loved to host friends—despite the cramped quarters. I like making granola when guests come to stay. I set it on the counter in a big glass jar the night before with a note inviting my guests to dig in if they wake up before I do. There's no better feeling than welcoming your loved ones to your new home.

MAKES 5 CUPS [500 G] GRANOLA

½ cup [110 g] coconut oil

¼ cup [80 g] maple syrup

2 cups [200 g] old-fashioned rolled oats

1 cup [100 g] unsweetened flaked coconut

1 cup [120 g] chopped raw hazelnuts

½ cup [50 g] sliced almonds

¼ tsp Maldon sea salt

½ cup [80 g] diced dried apricots

½ cup [70 g] diced dried cherries

Preheat the oven to 325°F [165°C]. Line a baking sheet with parchment paper and set aside.

In a large bowl, stir together the coconut oil and maple syrup to combine. Add the oats, coconut, hazelnuts, almonds, and salt. Stir until all ingredients are evenly coated. Pour onto the prepared baking sheet and spread evenly.

Bake for 25 to 30 minutes or until golden brown, stirring every 10 minutes. The coconut pieces will burn quickly, so when they are golden brown, remove the baking sheet from the oven.

Let the granola cool for several minutes. Stir in the apricots and cherries. Cool completely and store the granola in an airtight container where it will keep for about 10 days.

LEFTOVERS ARE A GOOD THING

This granola will stay fresh and crunchy for a long time. If you can't eat it all within 10 days or so, freeze it (for several months)! Just let it thaw for about 10 minutes at room temperature before eating.

DO YOUR THING

Swap out any of the nuts or dried fruit for your favorites. Swap out the maple syrup for honey if that's more your thing. A flavorless oil, such as vegetable, is a fine substitution for the coconut oil.

MAKE IT A MEAL

There are so many ways to enjoy this granola. I love it with fresh fruit and yogurt, in a kale salad, with a banana and peanut butter, or sprinkled over sorbet or ice cream.

Smoothies

Smoothies are the best solution when you have only a few minutes to throw something together and know you need to eat on the move. I buy recyclable cups and lids so we can drink our smoothies on the way to wherever we're headed, and toss the trash when finished.

Almond-Banana Smoothie

This smoothie is creamy, nutty, slightly sweet, and packed with nutrients that will help you feel alert, energetic, and ready for the day.

SERVES 2 AS A SNACK, 1 AS A MEAL

1 cup [120 g] ice cubes

1 large ripe banana

1 cup [240 ml] almond milk

2 Tbsp almond butter

1 Medjool date, pitted

½ tsp vanilla extract

¼ tsp almond extract

Combine all ingredients in a blender and blend on high speed until completely smooth, 20 to 30 seconds.

MAKE AHEAD

If I know our mornings will be really frantic, I'll throw all of my smoothie ingredients except the liquid into a large glass and put it all in the freezer so I can quickly dump them, plus the liquid ingredients, into the blender. I pour the smoothie straight back into the same glass and run out the door.

DO YOUR THING

In place of almond butter, use your favorite kind of nut or seed butter. Or, swap in 2 Tbsp raw nuts (such as cashews) that have been soaked in water overnight.

BUY SMART

If your bananas are starting to go bad, cut them up and freeze them for smoothies. Keep them frozen in an airtight container or resealable plastic freezer bag for several months.

Green Piña Colada Smoothie

This smoothie is a fresh, health-conscious, booze-free riff on my favorite vacation drink. Why can't every day feel like a honeymoon?

SERVES 2 AS A SNACK, 1 AS A MEAL

½ cup [120 ml] coconut milk

1½ cups [360 ml] cold water

1 cup [140 g] frozen pineapple

1 cup [140 g] frozen peaches

1 cup [120 g] ice cubes

½ cup [78 g] frozen spinach

2 Tbsp fresh lemon juice (from about 1 lemon)

1 Tbsp honey

Shake the coconut milk firmly before opening to combine the liquids with the solids because they naturally separate in the can.

Combine all ingredients in a blender and blend on high speed until completely smooth, 20 to 30 seconds.

LEFTOVERS ARE A GOOD THING

Tightly wrap the leftover coconut milk in the can with plastic wrap and use within 1 week. Stir it into a soup for dairy-free creaminess or try the Coconut Milk Shrimp (page 151) or Red Curry Mussels (page 150). Can't use it all within the week? Freeze it in an ice cube tray and add a cube or two to smoothies.

DO YOUR THING

Ditch the spinach and add a shot of rum—it's 5 o'clock somewhere!

BUY SMART

Depending on the season, it can be more cost-friendly to buy fresh fruit and chop it and freeze it yourself.

Berry and Cashew Cream Parfaits

The grab-and-go parfaits sold at your local coffee shop are easy, yes, but are a less-than-ideal choice for fueling your busy day—and can be tough on the budget, as well. Typically packed with sugary dairy yogurts, sugary (and soggy!) granola, and some mix of mushy fruit, they'll boost your energy in the short term but leave you crashing midmorning from your sugar high. With a bit of prep, you can create these protein-packed parfaits at home quicker (and cheaper) than you could check out at the coffee shop. Cashew cream is a great substitute when you crave something creamy and luscious but are trying to cut down on dairy. Make this cashew cream on a Sunday night and use it all week long to assemble these parfaits in just seconds.

MAKES 6 PARFAITS

FOR THE LEMON-VANILLA CASHEW CREAM
MAKES ABOUT 3½ CUPS [840 ML]

2 cups [280 g] whole raw cashews

1½ cups [360 ml] cold water

Zest of 1 lemon

Juice of 1 lemon

2 Tbsp honey

1 tsp vanilla extract

Pinch of kosher salt

FOR THE FRUIT SALAD
MAKES 6 CUPS [800 G]

2 cups [280 g] fresh blueberries

2 cups [280 g] hulled and quartered fresh strawberries

2 cups [240 g] fresh blackberries

2 Tbsp fresh lemon juice (from about 1 lemon)

2 tsp honey

6 Tbsp [36 g] store-bought granola or Hazeznut-Maple Granola (page 27)

To make the lemon-vanilla cashew cream: Place the cashews in a small bowl and cover them with cold water. Cover the bowl and refrigerate for at least 8 hours. Drain and rinse the cashews.

In a blender, combine the drained cashews, 1¼ cups [300 ml] of the cold water, the lemon zest, lemon juice, honey, vanilla, and salt. Blend on high speed for 2 minutes until smooth, scraping down the sides of the jar a couple of times as you go. If needed, add the remaining ¼ cup cold water, a little at a time, to achieve your desired consistency.

To make the fruit salad: In a large bowl, toss the blueberries, strawberries, and blackberries with the lemon juice and honey to combine.

To make the parfaits: Place ½ cup [65 g] of fruit salad in a cup or bowl. Top with ¼ cup [60 g] of cashew cream. Repeat layering one more time. Top each with 1 Tbsp granola.

To store for later use, transfer the fruit salad and cashew cream into separate airtight containers and keep refrigerated for up to 5 days.

LEFTOVERS ARE A GOOD THING

This recipe makes a lot of cashew cream; it's necessary for the batch to be this big to blend it to the right consistency. The good news: It's not just great for breakfast. Serve a big bowl of berries with a dollop of cashew cream for a decadent but nutritious dessert! It's also great over pancakes or waffles.

DO YOUR THING

Cashew cream is just as delicious as a savory cream as it is a sweet cream. Forego the vanilla and honey, and add a dollop of lemony cashew cream to savory grain bowls such as the Rainbow Veggie Bowls with Lemon Tahini Dressing (page 88).

BUY SMART

Buy precut fruit salad at the grocery store instead of making your own. Toss in a little fresh lemon juice to liven it up.

Ricotta Toast with Strawberry Rose Chia Jam

"Gourmet" toast has taken the country by storm. My Strawberry Rose Chia Jam will give you a really special new use for chia seeds, along with fancying up your usual toast for breakfast. When combined with strawberry purée, chia seeds gelatinize into a jam-like consistency that maintains the freshness of the strawberries since it requires zero cooking. Make the jam in advance, and on a busy morning you can throw this together quickly, or make a big platter of toast bites for a cozy brunch spread for two.

SERVES 2

FOR THE ROSE CHIA JAM

1 lb [455 g] fresh or frozen strawberries, stemmed and hulled

¼ cup [60 ml] fresh lemon juice (from about 2 lemons)

1 Tbsp maple syrup

¾ tsp rose water

3 Tbsp chia seeds

FOR THE RICOTTA TOAST

¼ cup [60 g] fresh ricotta cheese

2 large slices rustic bread, lightly toasted

To make the rose chia jam: In a high-powered blender, combine the strawberries, lemon juice, maple syrup, and rose water. Blend until smooth, 15 to 30 seconds. Pour the strawberry purée into a sealable container, add the chia seeds, and stir to combine. Refrigerate for at least 12 hours to gel.

To assemble the toast: Smear half the ricotta over each slice of toast. Spoon 1 Tbsp or so of jam over the top. Serve immediately.

LEFTOVERS ARE A GOOD THING

This recipe makes extra jam. Serve it over ice cream, with yogurt and granola, with Sweet Potato Biscuits (page 133), or on a cheeseboard.

SEASONALITY

Swap 1 lb [455 g] of any seasonal (or frozen) fruit for the strawberries.

SPECIAL INGREDIENT

Now that you have chia seeds in the pantry, make Raspberry-Coconut Chia Pudding (page 36)! You can even add a scoop of this jam to it.

Raspberry-Coconut Chia Pudding

Chia puddings can vary vastly—from fresh, fruity, and wonderful to slimy, icky, almost bizarre. I'm happy to say this pudding is the former. Chia seeds are stirred into a purée of yogurt, coconut milk, and strawberries, giving this chia pudding a creamy consistency. Don't like coconut? Partner loves nuts? Get creative and use any topping you like that will start the day with a smile.

SERVES 2

¾ cup [180 g] plain yogurt

½ cup [120 ml] coconut milk

½ cup [60 g] strawberries (fresh or frozen)

2 tsp maple syrup

½ tsp vanilla extract

3 Tbsp chia seeds

1 tsp coconut oil

¼ cup [20 g] coconut flakes

⅛ tsp kosher salt

In a blender, combine the yogurt, coconut milk, strawberries, maple syrup, and vanilla. Blend until smooth. Pour the yogurt mixture into a large airtight container and stir in the chia seeds. Refrigerate for at least 12 hours.

In a small skillet over medium heat, warm the coconut oil. Add the coconut flakes and salt. Toast for 3 to 5 minutes, stirring frequently, or until golden brown. Transfer to a paper towel-lined plate to cool.

Divide the chia pudding between two bowls, sprinkle on the toasted coconut or any other desired toppings, and enjoy immediately! Store any leftover coconut in an airtight container at room temperature for up to 4 days.

SEASONALITY

Try mango, raspberries, blueberries, cherries, or whatever fruit you have on hand in place of the strawberries.

DO YOUR THING

One of the best desserts I've ever had was a really creamy chia pudding surrounded by crème anglaise (basically, melted vanilla ice cream). Try serving this as an after-dinner sweet; it should be enough for four as a dessert, and a good reason to linger with friends around the table.

5-Minute Caprese Breakfast Tacos

Hardboiled eggs are a quick protein powerhouse. They can be cooked days in advance and stored in the refrigerator for a ready breakfast or snack. Geroge and I are taco addicts, and much to our satisfaction, we've found that boiled eggs also make a *delightful* breakfast taco filling, meaning we can have award-worthy breakfast tacos on our plates in under 5 minutes. If you or your breakfast partner likes runny yolks, softboil the eggs and let them come to room temperature before chopping.

SERVES 2

5 tsp olive oil

Four 6-in [15-cm] corn or flour tortillas

⅓ cup [25 g] shredded mozzarella cheese

4 large hardboiled or softboiled eggs, chopped

¼ cup [40 g] chopped cherry tomatoes

¼ cup [5 g] fresh basil chiffonade (see Cooking School, page 40) or microgreens

Maldon sea salt

Freshly ground black pepper

In a large nonstick skillet over medium-high heat, heat 2 tsp of the olive oil. Cook the tortillas for 1 to 2 minutes on one side until lightly browned. Flip, sprinkle with cheese, and cook for about 2 minutes more, until the cheese is lightly melted and the second side is lightly browned. Divide the tortillas between two plates.

Top the tortillas with eggs, cherry tomatoes, and basil. Drizzle each taco with some of the remaining olive oil and season with salt and pepper. Serve immediately.

LEFTOVERS ARE A GOOD THING

You can pretty much wrap anything in a tortilla with eggs and call it a breakfast taco. Leftover peach gochujang sauce is delicious drizzled over the top. The last bit of Colorful Sausage and Peppers (page 40), Grilled Corn and Tahini Salad (page 224), or bruschetta would make tasty breakfast taco fillings as well.

DO YOUR THING

Substitute fresh salsa and avocado for the mozzarella, tomatoes, and basil for a Mexican breakfast taco.

No Recipe Saucy Baked Eggs

George calls me the queen of leftovers. He is constantly in awe of the way I can turn last night's leftovers into the next morning's breakfast feast. Leftover Harissa Braised Short Ribs (page 205) and sauce, Baked Meatball sauce (page 198), and Mushroom Ragu (page 162) are all excellent candidates for this "no recipe" recipe. Some version of this recipe goes down at our house at least once a week. As an ongoing strategy, it's good to invest the time in a few meals that keep on giving throughout the week, meaning less time in the kitchen and more time with the person you just married! After the initial assembly, it's really hands-off, so even on a busy morning it's a cinch to prepare a nutritious meal.

SERVES 2

1½ cups [360 ml] leftover or store-bought sauce of choice

2 to 4 large eggs

Kosher salt

Freshly ground black pepper

2 Tbsp cheese, such as mozzarella, feta, or goat cheese

Chopped fresh herbs of choice

2 slices toast

Position a rack in the top third of the oven and preheat the broiler.

In an 8-in [20-cm] ovenproof skillet over medium heat, warm the sauce. When warmed, use a spatula to make divots in the sauce (one per egg). Crack the eggs into the divots. Season the eggs with salt and pepper and cook for several minutes, until the bottoms of the whites are set. Sprinkle the cheese over the sauce and egg whites (don't put it on top of the yolks), and transfer the skillet to the oven.

Broil for 2 to 4 minutes, until the whites are set and the yolks are cooked to your desired doneness. Remove the skillet from the oven, garnish the dish with fresh herbs, and enjoy digging in with slices of toast—straight out of the skillet!

DO YOUR THING

To get your creative juices flowing, tomatillo salsa with Cotija cheese and cilantro, vodka sauce with goat cheese and parsley, and pizza sauce with mozzarella and basil are all winning sauce-cheese combos.

COOKING SCHOOL

Guests in town? This recipe can easily be doubled or tripled in a larger skillet and will be sure to please. If you don't have leftover sauce, use a really good jarred tomato sauce. Be sure to serve it with lots of good bread for sopping up the sauce.

Colorful Sausage and Peppers

Here, I've given the classic Italian-American dish of sautéed sausage and peppers a breakfast makeover by swapping spicy Italian sausage for leaner chicken sausage. This recipe makes a large batch that reheats really well for days.

SERVES 2 GENEROUSLY

1 tsp olive oil

2 precooked chicken sausage links (in an herby flavor; garlic herb or basil pesto are popular), cut on the diagonal into ¼-in- [6-mm-] thick slices, to make long, thin pieces

½ small yellow onion, cut into ¼-in [6-mm] slices

1 large red bell pepper, cut into ¼-in [6-mm] slices

1 large yellow bell pepper, cut into ¼-in [6-mm] slices

½ tsp kosher salt

½ tsp garlic powder

¼ tsp red pepper flakes

2 Tbsp apple cider vinegar

Poached Eggs (page 48; optional)

1 cup [20 g] plus 2 Tbsp chiffonade fresh basil leaves (see Cooking School)

Maldon sea salt

Freshly ground black pepper

In a large nonstick skillet over medium-high heat, warm the olive oil. Swirl to coat the pan. Add the sausage pieces and cook for 1 minute per side until just lightly browned.

Add the onion, red bell pepper, yellow bell pepper, kosher salt, garlic powder, and red pepper flakes. Cook for 5 minutes, stirring occasionally. Add the vinegar and cook for 2 to 3 minutes more, until the vegetables soften and have browned but still maintain a bit of body and their vibrant colors.

Meanwhile, poach the eggs (if using).

Remove the skillet from the heat and stir in 1 cup [20 g] of the basil. Transfer the pepper mixture to two bowls, and place one poached egg (if using) in each bowl. Garnish with the remaining 2 Tbsp basil. Season with sea salt and pepper.

MAKE AHEAD

The onion, bell peppers, and sausage can be cooked in advance, cooled, and refrigerated. When you're ready to eat, reheat them in a skillet over medium heat for 4 to 6 minutes (or for 30 seconds in the microwave), stir in the basil, and top with the eggs, if desired.

MAKE IT A MEAL

For lunch or dinner, serve over your favorite grain or pasta, add another bell pepper and sausage link, and forego the eggs if you aren't into eggs after breakfast.

COOKING SCHOOL

To chiffonade basil, stack the leaves together, roll tightly, and cut across into very thin slices.

Mushroom, Kale, and Sausage Personal Frittatas

When we have a really busy week ahead of us, I know that meal prep is crucial if we want to eat healthy. Mini muffin tin frittatas are always in rotation for quick, microwave-and-go breakfasts. Even if we can't sit down for a quick breakfast together on a busy morning, just heating up a premade breakfast for the other is such a caring gesture and easy demonstration of love.

MAKES 6 PERSONAL FRITTATAS

5⅓ oz [152 g] Italian sausage (1 normal-size link), casing removed

1 cup [20 g] finely chopped kale

½ cup [30 g] diced mixed mushrooms

½ tsp kosher salt

8 large eggs

¼ cup [60 ml] whole milk yogurt or milk

¼ tsp red pepper flakes

2 oz [55 g] Gruyère cheese, cut into very small cubes

Preheat the oven to 350°F [180°C] and position a rack in the upper third of the oven. Butter a standard size 6-cup muffin tin thoroughly.

In a large skillet over medium heat, cook the sausage for 2 to 3 minutes, breaking it up into small pieces with a wooden spoon. When the sausage is nearly cooked and the skillet is very greasy, add the kale, mushrooms, and ¼ tsp of the salt. Stirring frequently, cook for 3 to 4 minutes, until the mushrooms are cooked through and the kale is wilted. Remove the skillet from the heat. Use a clean paper towel to pat the sausage mixture and remove as much grease as possible.

In a large bowl, whisk the eggs, yogurt, remaining ¼ tsp salt, and the red pepper flakes.

Divide the sausage mixture and Gruyère cubes among the prepared 6 muffin cups. Pour the egg mixture into each cup so it just covers the ingredients. Put the muffin tin on a baking sheet and into the oven.

Cook for 17 to 20 minutes, until the frittatas puff and the eggs are set. Enjoy immediately, or remove the mini frittatas from their cups and cool completely on a rack before refrigerating in an airtight container for up to 4 days. Reheat gently in the microwave in 10-second intervals.

TOOL TIP

No muffin tin? Cook these in small ovenproof bowls, or just pour everything into a small nonstick ovenproof skillet, bake, and slice into individual portions.

MAKE IT A MEAL

If I'm honest, I mostly eat these directly off a paper towel in my car on the way to whatever meeting I'm late for. But when I do enjoy them on a plate, in the comfort of my own home, I love pairing them with a green salad dressed with leftover Apple Cider Vinaigrette (page 91), or smashing them a bit and sandwiching them between two slices of toasted bread with a splash of hot sauce for the easiest breakfast sandwich ever.

BUY SMART

The meat counters at most major grocery stores sell sausage by the link. You need only one link for this recipe, so that may be a smarter way to buy if you don't have an immediate use for the others in a full package.

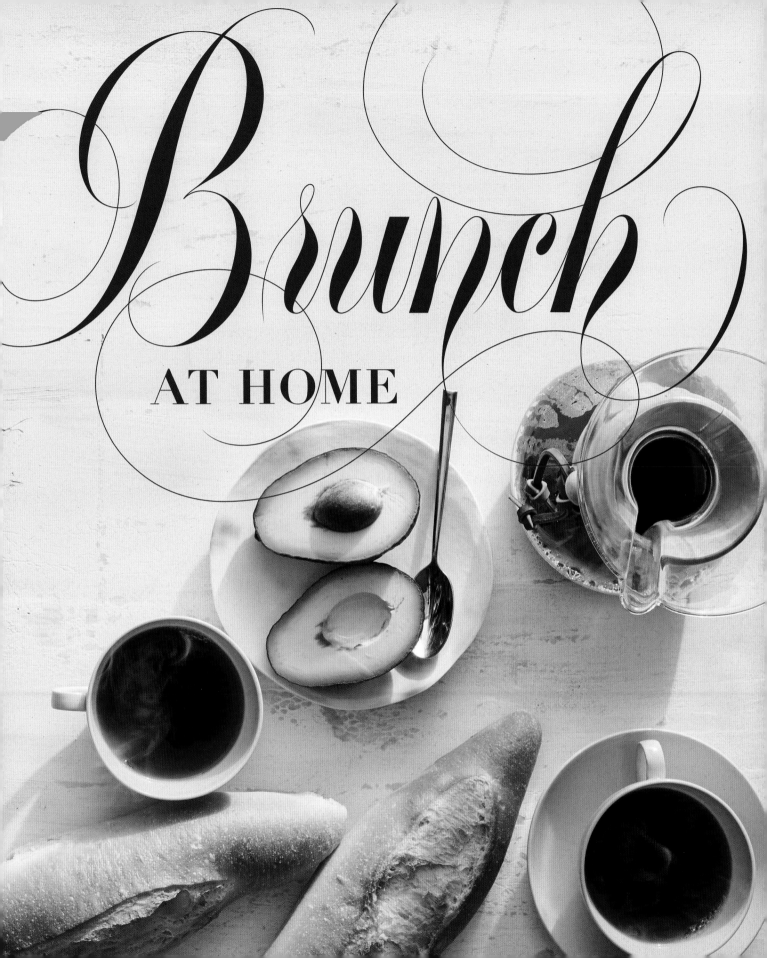

Brunch

AT HOME

In our house, there's a *huge* difference between breakfast at 7 a.m. on a Wednesday morning and breakfast at 10 a.m. on a Saturday morning. Weekend mornings are a chance for us to slow down, enjoy a home-brewed latte (or two . . . or three . . .) and relish the ability to laze around with zero agenda. George handles the caffeine and tunes while I scrounge through the fridge and rummage through cookbooks I've earmarked, searching for the perfect recipe to fuel our day together.

The following recipes are a few of our favorite healthy (Cauliflower Steak and Eggs with Harissa Yogurt, page 53, and Sweet-and-Spicy Citrus Salad, page 64), and not-as-healthy (Spinach and Artichoke Skillet Strata, page 56, and Crispy Smashed Potatoes, page 52) ways to ease into a laid-back weekend morning. Some Sundays were made for meals that make you want to fall immediately back to sleep, while others demand a dish that revs you up to tackle a six-mile hike. You'll find a mix of both to nourish your days spent together.

How to Cook Eggs

Eggs are such an easy and quick (and newlywed-budget-friendly!) solution to pack a ton of vitamins and protein into any meal. Here are several ways to cook a perfect egg. It's important to pay attention to the cooking descriptors (i.e., "cook until the edges are brown"), because everyone's stove is slightly different and heat is the most important thing here.

Soft-Fried Eggs

SERVE 1 OR 2 EGGS PER PERSON

1 Tbsp unsalted butter

2 to 4 large eggs

Kosher salt

In a nonstick skillet over low heat, melt the butter. It should melt very slowly. Swirl to coat the pan. Crack the eggs into the skillet and sprinkle with a bit of salt. They should take about 5 minutes to cook and the whites should not brown. Gently poke the whites around the yolk. When they are no longer runny, the egg is ready.

Crispy Olive Oil–Fried Eggs

SERVE 1 OR 2 EGGS PER PERSON

1 Tbsp olive oil

2 to 4 large eggs

Kosher salt

In a nonstick skillet over low heat, heat the olive oil until it shimmers and is nearly smoking. Carefully crack the eggs into the skillet and sprinkle with a bit of salt. The eggs will bubble up and pop in the pan and the edges will turn golden brown. Gently poke the whites around the yolk. When they are no longer runny, the egg is ready.

Hard-Boiled Eggs

SERVE 1 OR 2 EGGS PER PERSON

. . . .

2 to 4 large eggs

Place the eggs in a pot with a lid and cover with 1 in [2.5 cm] of cold water. Place the pot over high heat, bring to a boil, cover the pot, and immediately remove it from the heat. Set aside for 10 minutes. Carefully drain and transfer the eggs to ice water to cool. "Shocking" the eggs in this fashion stops them from overcooking and makes them easier to peel. Gently crack and peel under running water.

Soft-Boiled Eggs

SERVE 1 OR 2 EGGS PER PERSON

. . . .

2 to 4 large eggs

Add 4 in [10 cm] of water to a pot and bring to a rolling boil over high heat. Reduce the heat to medium. When it is gently boiling, use a slotted spoon to lower the eggs gently into the water, one by one. Cook for 7 minutes uncovered. Carefully drain and transfer the eggs to ice water to cool completely. "Shocking" the eggs in this fashion stops them from overcooking and makes them easier to peel. Gently crack and peel under running water.

Poached Eggs

SERVE 1 OR 2 EGGS PER PERSON

. . . .

2 to 4 large eggs

1 Tbsp white vinegar

To a large saucepan with a lid, add 2 in [5 cm] of water and the white vinegar. Bring to a boil over high heat. One by one, crack each egg into a small cup and carefully (and gently) pour the egg from the cup into the water. Remove the pan from the heat, cover it, and let the eggs poach in the hot water for 3 to 5 minutes, until they reach your desired doneness. To check the doneness, gently poke the egg: If it is soft, it's still runny inside; if it's firm, the yolk is cooked through. Remove with a slotted spoon.

Simple Omelet

SERVE 1 OR 2 EGGS PER PERSON

1 Tbsp unsalted butter

3 large eggs

Kosher salt

Freshly ground black pepper

3 to 4 Tbsp [weight varies] of your favorite fillings, such as shredded cheese, chopped tomato, diced bell pepper or onion, etc.

In an 8-in [20-cm] nonstick skillet over medium heat, melt the butter. In a small bowl, whisk the eggs, seasoned with salt and pepper, until combined. When the butter melts, add the eggs to the skillet and use a spatula to move them around quickly, for 10 seconds, scraping the bottom and sides of the skillet quickly and thoroughly. When the omelet is only slightly runny on top, use a large spatula to flip it by tilting the skillet toward you as you gently shimmy the spatula underneath and quickly lift and flip the omelet. Immediately remove the skillet from the heat. Place the fillings on half of the omelet and fold the other half over them. Your fillings don't need to be warm; if you let the omelet sit for 1 to 2 minutes before sliding it onto a plate and serving, it should heat them through.

Marbled Eggs

SERVE 1 OR 2 EGGS PER PERSON

1 Tbsp unsalted butter

2 to 4 large eggs

In an 8-in [20-cm] skillet with a lid over medium heat, melt the butter. Crack an egg or two directly into the skillet. Pop the yolk with a fork and use the fork to drag the yolk through the whites and the whites through the yolks, creating a "marbled" effect. Repeat with additional eggs, as needed. Cover the skillet and cook for 2 to 3 minutes, until the whites and yolks are set. Marbled eggs are great for breakfast sandwiches or in place of a fried egg for those who don't like runny yolks but who also don't love biting into an entire chalky egg yolk.

Slow-Scrambled Eggs

SERVE 1 OR 2 EGGS PER PERSON

2 to 4 large eggs

1 Tbsp unsalted butter

Kosher salt

Freshly ground black pepper

In a cold, medium skillet, crack the eggs and add the butter. Place the skillet over low heat and whisk for 30 seconds. Every 30 seconds for the next 5 to 7 minutes, whisk the eggs for a couple of seconds. When they still look slightly undercooked, remove the skillet from the heat, season with salt and pepper, and whisk for several seconds. Quickly transfer to plates to stop the cooking.

Almond Earl Grey Latte

Home-brewed lattes are a luxury reserved for slow, lazy weekend mornings. They're easy enough to make, but milk frothing never seems to make the cut on busy weekdays when we're both rushing out the door. Saturdays at our house often begin with sipping these lattes out of portable mugs while on a walk with our dog, Hooper.

SERVES 2

2 Earl Grey tea bags

1 Tbsp sugar

2 cups [480 ml] boiling water

¾ cup [180 ml] whole milk or unsweetened almond milk

½ tsp vanilla extract

¼ tsp almond extract

Divide the teabags and sugar between two large mugs. Pour 1 cup [240 ml] boiling water over each. Steep for 4 minutes. The tea should be very strong. Use a milk frother to steam the milk, and stir to blend. Stir half the milk, ¼ tsp of the vanilla, and ⅛ tsp of the almond extract into each mug. Enjoy immediately.

TOOL TIP

If you don't have a milk frother, add the brewed tea, warmed milk, and remaining ingredients to a high-powered blender. Blend on high speed for 20 seconds. It won't be exactly the same, but it will be frothy and delicious.

DO YOUR THING

Bonus points for using homemade almond or cashew milk (see Vanilla Cashew Coffee Creamer, facing page). It won't froth as mightily as whole milk, but it will be delicious!

Vanilla Cashew Coffee Creamer

I am a serial over creamer. By the time coffee is fit for my consumption, it's practically white. For many years, I was hooked on artificially flavored creamers (hazelnut! French vanilla! peppermint mocha!), but after we were married, George was horrified to find the preservative-packed stuff in our newly shared refrigerator and helped me kick the habit. This far more nutritious coffee creamer has the added benefit of being packed with protein and fiber, which helps keep you energized longer. Warning: You may find your partner sneaking sips straight out of the container.

MAKES 1½ CUPS [360 ML]

½ cup [70 g] raw whole cashews

1½ cups [360 ml] water

1 Medjool date, pitted

½ tsp vanilla extract

Pinch of kosher salt

In a small bowl, combine the cashews with 2 in [5 cm] of water. Soak overnight, or for at least 8 hours. Drain and rinse the cashews.

In a blender, combine the cashews, water, date, vanilla, and salt. Blend for about 45 seconds on the highest speed, until completely smooth. Transfer to an airtight container and keep refrigerated for up to 5 days.

LEFTOVERS ARE A GOOD THING

If you can't finish all the creamer within 5 days, freeze it into ice cubes in an ice cube tray. Pop one cube into your hot coffee; as it melts it will cream your coffee and cool it to the perfect drinking temperature.

DO YOUR THING

To make an almond coffee creamer, swap ½ cup [70 g] raw almonds for the cashews, and strain the milk through a fine-mesh strainer before storing. (Almonds are more fibrous than cashews and require straining.)

BUY SMART

Find cashews and dates in the bulk bins at most major grocery stores. No need to buy more than you need!

Crispy Smashed Potatoes

These potatoes would be just as welcome on a dinner table as on a brunch table. Experiment with your own seasonings: a bit of curry powder or garam masala with fresh cilantro for an Indian direction, or cumin, chili powder, and scallions for a Southwestern kick. Also try them with a dollop of Harissa Yogurt (facing page).

SERVES 2

1 lb [445 g] baby Yukon Gold potatoes or other small potato

Vegetable oil for frying, or other neutral oil with a high smoke point

1 fresh rosemary sprig

6 garlic cloves, peeled and smashed

½ tsp Maldon sea salt

¼ tsp red pepper flakes

2 Tbsp finely chopped fresh parsley

½ cup [15 g] grated Parmesan cheese

Bring a large pot of water to a boil over high heat. Add the potatoes and cook for 20 minutes, or until easily pierced with a fork. Drain and let them cool for at least 30 minutes. You can put them in the refrigerator to speed this up. It's very important to let the potatoes cool; they will fall apart when you smash them if you don't.

Using your hand or a pot, gently press down on each potato until it's about ½ in [1.25 cm] thick.

To your largest skillet over medium-high heat, add ½ in [1.25 cm] oil. Drop a rosemary leaf in—it will begin sizzling immediately when the oil is hot enough.

Add the garlic to the oil and fry for about 1 minute per side, until golden brown. Use a slotted spoon to transfer to a paper towel-lined plate.

Drop the rosemary sprig into the oil for about 45 seconds. Transfer to the paper towel-lined plate.

Add the potatoes to the hot oil in batches. Fry about 3 minutes per side, until golden brown. Transfer to the paper towel-lined plate and lightly pat the tops

of the potatoes with another paper towel to remove any excess oil.

Transfer everything to a serving dish, scattering the fried garlic over the top. Use your hands to crumble the fried rosemary over the potatoes. Sprinkle with the salt, red pepper flakes, parsley, and Parmesan.

LEFTOVERS ARE A GOOD THING

For larger batches, forego frying; it'll take too long. Place the smashed potatoes on an aluminum foil–lined baking sheet and drizzle with olive oil. Roast at 450°F [230°C] for about 30 minutes, until golden brown and crispy.

MAKE AHEAD

The potatoes can be boiled up to 2 days in advance. Refrigerate them until you're ready to fry them. Don't refrigerate them between frying and serving, because they will lose their crispiness; instead keep them warm on a sheet pan in a 200°F [95°C] oven.

Cauliflower Steak and Eggs with Harissa Yogurt

When I first met George, he ascribed to the "no meat, no meal" way of thought. It didn't take long for me to convince him that, when prepared properly, a vegetarian meal could satisfy his needs just as well as a juicy steak. This dish is packed with texture from the soft, roasted cauliflower, to the crispy, bread crumb-coated fried eggs, to the creamy, spicy yogurt. I love serving this vegetarian "steak and eggs" for breakfast—it's so unexpected.

SERVES 2, WITH LEFTOVER CAULIFLOWER

FOR THE CAULIFLOWER STEAKS

1 head cauliflower, leaves trimmed from the base

1 Tbsp extra-virgin olive oil

½ tsp garlic powder

½ tsp kosher salt

¼ tsp freshly ground black pepper

FOR THE HARISSA YOGURT

½ cup [120 g] Greek yogurt

1 Tbsp harissa

1 Tbsp fresh lemon juice (from about ½ lemon)

FOR THE CRISPY EGGS

1 Tbsp extra-virgin olive oil

¼ cup [15 g] panko bread crumbs

Kosher salt

Freshly ground black pepper

2 large eggs

2 Tbsp chopped fresh herbs of choice

Lemon wedges for serving

Preheat the oven to 400°F [200°C]. Line a baking sheet with aluminum foil.

To make the cauliflower steaks: Cut the cauliflower into 1-in- [2.5-cm-] thick "steaks": Place the base on your cutting board and carefully make 4 or 5 vertical cuts through the cauliflower head. Trim any florets that fall off into 1-in [2.5-cm] pieces. You'll probably make only 3 or 4 full "steaks" out of a single head of cauliflower. No worries—this is just as good with the florets.

Space the cauliflower steaks and florets evenly on the prepared baking sheet, drizzle with the olive oil, and season with the garlic powder, salt, and pepper. Place the baking sheet in the oven and cook for 20 minutes. Use a spatula to carefully flip the cauliflower and cook for 15 minutes more. Remove from the oven and set aside.

To make the harissa yogurt: In a small bowl, stir together the yogurt, harissa, and lemon juice. Divide

continued

the yogurt between two plates and use the back of a spoon to gently smear it into an oval shape. Place two cauliflower steaks (or some florets) over the harissa yogurt on each plate.

To make the crispy eggs: In a large nonstick skillet over medium heat, warm the olive oil. Add the bread crumbs, season with salt and pepper, and cook for about 30 seconds, stirring often, until the bread crumbs just begin to turn golden brown. Divide the bread crumbs into two 4-in- [10-cm-] wide flat piles. Gently crack one egg over each bread crumb pile. With a spatula, scoop up any bread crumbs not covered by the eggs and place them on top of the eggs. Cook the eggs for about 2 minutes, until the whites are almost set. Flip the eggs and immediately turn off the heat. Continue to cook the eggs in the hot skillet for 20 seconds more. Place the eggs on top of the cauliflower. Sprinkle with the herbs and serve immediately with a lemon wedge.

LEFTOVERS ARE A GOOD THING

Smear a spoonful of Harissa Yogurt on a slice of crusty bread and top with a fried egg and a shower of grated Parmesan. Snack time!

DO YOUR THING

No harissa in your pantry? Swap a few spoonfuls of salsa, pesto, or hummus, leftover Charred Poblano Romesco (page 202) or Beet Tzatziki (page 126) for the Harissa Yogurt. If you're feeling extra hungry, make two crispy eggs per person.

Spinach and Artichoke Skillet Strata

My mother is the queen of strata. Anytime she has guests sleeping under her roof, the savory aromas of a piping-hot strata and fresh coffee lure them to the kitchen in the morning. A good strata will make it seem as though you've been slaving away in the kitchen all morning, but the truth is, this dish is best when assembled the night before and simply baked in the morning.

Since most strata recipes feed many mouths, I created this skillet strata for two, perfect for a cozy Sunday morning at home. I borrowed the flavors of America's (and George's) favorite appetizer—spinach and artichoke dip—and packed them into this cheesy, decadent breakfast dish. Once you've mastered this recipe, experiment with different ingredients to make your own favorite strata creations. I like making a "Greek" strata with roasted red peppers, Kalamata olives, feta cheese, and artichoke hearts.

SERVES 2 TO 4

3 large eggs	1 cup [20 g] thawed drained chopped frozen spinach
1 cup [240 ml] whole milk	One (12-oz [340-g]) can whole artichoke hearts, rinsed, drained, and chopped
½ tsp garlic powder	½ cup [40 g] shredded mozzarella cheese
½ tsp kosher salt	¼ cup [8 g] grated Parmesan cheese
⅛ tsp cayenne pepper	¼ tsp red pepper flakes
5 or 6 thick sourdough bread slices, crusts removed, cut into 1-in [2.5-cm] squares	

Oil an 8-in [20-cm] nonstick skillet.

In a large bowl, whisk the eggs, milk, garlic powder, salt, and cayenne pepper for about 30 seconds, until well combined.

Evenly distribute half the bread cubes over the bottom of the skillet. Pour half the egg mixture over the top. Distribute the spinach, artichoke hearts, ¼ cup [20 g] of the mozzarella cheese, and the Parmesan cheese over the egg mixture. Top with the remaining bread cubes and remaining egg mixture. Sprinkle the remaining ¼ cup [20 g] mozzarella and the red pepper flakes over the top. Cover and refrigerate for at least 30 minutes, ideally overnight.

Preheat the oven to 350°F [180°C] at least 20 minutes before baking.

Bake the strata uncovered for about 30 minutes, until puffed and golden. Let stand for 5 minutes before slicing (allowing it to rest makes it easier to slice and serve).

MAKE AHEAD

This dish is actually best when assembled the night before! Throw it together while you're cooking dinner, refrigerate overnight, and bake it in the morning.

DO YOUR THING

If you have bread, milk, and eggs in your house, you can make a strata. Even a strata with random bits of left-over cheese as its only ingredient will be delicious. Use any kind of bread and any ingredients you think work together. Sausage, kale, and Gruyère is another favorite at our house.

COOKING SCHOOL

Take a cue from my mother: A strata is the absolute best way to feed breakfast to a crowd. Double, triple, or quadruple this recipe and cook it until it is no longer runny in the center when poked with a knife.

Sautéed Spinach with Baked Eggs and Feta

Two great things will come out of learning to cook this dish: First, you will learn to make a sautéed spinach side to rival any steakhouse. To do so, just serve the spinach after completing the first step. Second, you also learn you can pretty much crack eggs over any sautéed vegetable, bake it, and call it breakfast (or dinner!). Sautéed mushrooms, sautéed peppers and onions, and sautéed zucchini noodles all make perfect baked egg vessels. George is always amazed by what I can dig out of the bottom of the refrigerator, sauté, crack an egg over, and declare breakfast. Serve this dish with a slice of toast and call it a (good) morning.

SERVES 2 TO 4

1 Tbsp unsalted butter	½ tsp kosher salt
1 Tbsp olive oil	⅛ tsp smoked paprika
1 large garlic clove, thinly sliced	4 large eggs
1 large shallot, thinly sliced	2 oz [55 g] feta cheese, crumbled
12 oz [340 g] fresh spinach (about 12 cups)	Sliced avocado, Pickled Red Onions (page 82), chopped fresh herbs, and hot sauce for topping (optional)
1 tsp fresh lemon juice	

Preheat the oven to 350°F [180°C].

In a 12-in [30.5-cm] nonstick ovenproof skillet over medium heat, melt together the butter and olive oil. Add the garlic and shallot. Cook for about 4 minutes, stirring often, until soft and beginning to brown.

Working quickly, add the spinach to the skillet by the handful, tearing it with your hands first. You may have to cook the spinach down a bit between additions to fit more in the pan.

Add the lemon juice, salt, and paprika. Cook for 1 to 2 minutes, until the spinach is lightly wilted but still bright green. You want the spinach to maintain

a bit of body, as it will continue to cook in the oven. Remove the skillet from the heat.

Use the back of a spoon to make four wells in the spinach. Make sure you still have a layer of spinach covering the bottom of the pan, because you don't want the eggs to hit the pan directly. Carefully crack 1 egg into each well. Sprinkle the feta cheese over the spinach and egg whites, avoiding the yolks. Transfer the skillet to the middle rack in the oven and cook for 12 to 15 minutes, until the egg whites are set but the yolks are still runny. Remove from the oven and serve immediately, garnished with toppings of choice, if you like.

DO YOUR THING

Swap in any kind of greens here. Just adjust cooking times accordingly, because heartier greens such as kale and Swiss chard take longer to wilt.

COOKING SCHOOL

For an impressive brunch entrée, transfer the spinach to individual ramekins, crack an egg or two over the top, sprinkle feta over the whites, and bake according to the directions. If you plan to double or triple the recipe, cook the spinach in batches, transferring it to the ramekins as soon as it wilts.

BUY SMART

My grocery store sells 12-oz [340-g] bags of spinach, but yours might sell slightly larger or smaller bags. No worries if your bag isn't exactly 12 oz [340 g]. Spinach cooks down so much that exact quantities aren't important here.

Kimchi-Cheddar Egg Pancake

Kimchi, a spicy fermented cabbage condiment popular in Korea, and Cheddar cheese combine to create this fluffy, spicy, ultra-flavorful brunch entrée. If you're unfamiliar with kimchi, don't let that scare you away from this dish—my *very* Midwestern brother-in-law Nick claims this is the best thing I've ever made. I call this a brunch recipe, but it's also fantastic for lunch or dinner with a big leafy salad.

SERVES 2 TO 4

4 large eggs	¾ cup [105 g] all-purpose flour
¾ cup [180 ml] whole milk	1 cup [150 g] chopped and drained store-bought spicy kimchi
2 Tbsp unsalted butter, melted and slightly cooled, plus 1 Tbsp for cooking	¾ cup [60 g] grated sharp Cheddar cheese
½ tsp kosher salt	4 scallions, white and light green parts only, thinly sliced
½ tsp cayenne pepper (optional)	Bacon, avocado, more kimchi, Sriracha, chopped fresh soft herbs for topping (optional)
1 garlic clove, roughly chopped	

Place a 10-in [25-cm] ovenproof skillet (preferably cast iron) in the oven and preheat the oven to 450°F [230°C]. The skillet should heat for at least 15 minutes while you prepare the batter.

In a blender, combine the eggs, milk, 2 Tbsp of the melted butter, the salt, cayenne, garlic, and flour. Process at medium speed for 10 seconds, or until just combined. Do not overblend.

Add the kimchi, Cheddar, and scallions and pulse on low speed once or twice just to incorporate the ingredients. Be careful not to overblend and lose the texture!

Carefully remove the skillet from the oven and add the remaining 1 Tbsp butter. Swirl to coat the skillet. Quickly pour the batter into the skillet, using a fork to distribute the cheese and kimchi evenly. Return the skillet to the center of the oven. Bake for 20 to 25 minutes, until puffed and brown around the edges. Remove and let sit for about 5 minutes before serving with toppings as desired.

LEFTOVERS ARE A GOOD THING

This dish is great for brunch with friends, but it also reheats really well for just the two of you. Microwave in 15-second intervals until heated through.

SPECIAL INGREDIENT

Use leftover kimchi to make Veggie Bibimbap (page 165).

DO YOUR THING

To simplify the flavors of this dish into a quick breakfast for two, scramble four eggs with 2 Tbsp grated Cheddar cheese and 2 Tbsp chopped kimchi in a medium skillet over medium heat.

Banana-Oat Pancakes

We always seem to crave pancakes after a particularly late night out. But after said late night out, who wants to brush their hair, put on real clothes, and run to the grocery store? I don't typically have milk or buttermilk (essential pancake ingredients) in my fridge, so on one particularly lazy, hazy morning when George was in grad school, I came up with this pancake recipe that uses ingredients I almost always have on hand. These pancakes satisfy that sweet, indulgent, carby craving, while simultaneously nourishing with vitamins and nutrients from the oats, bananas, and Greek yogurt.

SERVES 2

½ cup [70 g] all-purpose flour

½ cup [60 g] oat flour

½ tsp kosher salt

½ tsp baking powder

½ tsp baking soda

1½ tsp ground cinnamon

2 very ripe large bananas

1 cup [240 g] Greek yogurt

2 large eggs

2 Tbsp unsalted butter, melted and cooled slightly

1 Tbsp plus 1 tsp maple syrup, plus more for serving

1 tsp vanilla extract

1 or 2 Tbsp vegetable oil

2 Tbsp finely chopped toasted walnuts

Preheat the oven to 200°F [95°C]. Line a baking sheet with parchment paper.

In a large bowl, use a fork to combine the all-purpose flour, oat flour, salt, baking powder, baking soda, and cinnamon.

In a medium bowl, use a fork to mash 1 banana. Whisk in the yogurt, eggs, melted butter, maple syrup, and vanilla.

Add the banana mixture to the flour mixture and stir to combine. When they are combined, stop stirring! If you overmix the batter, your pancakes won't be light and fluffy.

In a large nonstick skillet, griddle, or cast iron pan over medium heat, warm 1 Tbsp vegetable oil until it shimmers. Pour the batter into the skillet in 2-Tbsp portions to form pancakes that are roughly 3 in [7 cm] wide. When small bubbles form on the surface of the pancakes (this should take about 3 minutes), they're ready to flip—but keep an eye on them, because all stovetops are different. If your pancakes burn before bubbles form, turn the heat down. Flip the pancakes and cook the second side for 1 to 2 minutes, or until golden brown. Transfer the cooked pancakes to the prepared baking sheet and keep warm in the oven until ready to serve. Continue making pancakes until you've used all the batter. Add more vegetable oil to the pan, as needed.

Cut the remaining banana into ¼-in [6-mm] slices. Divide the pancakes between two plates and top with banana slices, walnuts, and maple syrup.

LEFTOVERS ARE A GOOD THING

Wrap cooled leftover pancakes individually in plastic wrap, put in large resealable plastic bags, and freeze for up to 2 months. To reheat, microwave in 30 second intervals until warmed through.

TOOL TIP

If you have a wet ingredient measuring cup (the glass ones with handles), this is a great place to use it. Transfer your pancake batter to the measuring cup for easy pouring into your skillet.

DO YOUR THING

Swap in 1 cup [240 g] of yogurt, sour cream, crème fraîche, or buttermilk [240 ml] for the Greek yogurt. Try ½ cup [100 g] of mashed sweet potatoes in place of the banana. If you don't like walnuts, swap in your favorite nut, or dust the pancakes with powdered sugar instead.

BUY SMART

If you have oats in your pantry, there's no need to buy oat flour. Just pulverize ½ cup [50 g] of old-fashioned rolled oats in a blender or food processor. It won't be as fine as oat flour, but it'll add a nice texture to the pancakes.

Sweet-and-Spicy Citrus Salad

While George was in graduate school in Palo Alto, California, we lived in a tiny house with the most enormous yard you've ever seen. It was full of fruit trees—figs, oranges, grapefruits, lemons, limes . . . you name it. The trees produced so much fruit in winter months we couldn't even begin to consume it all. Instead of bringing a bottle of wine to dinner at a friend's house, we started showing up with armloads of citrus. Some iteration of this sweet, spicy, crunchy, tangy salad was, and still is, on repeat at our house all winter long. This salad is visually stunning when you have a varied assortment of citrus colors and sizes, but it's wonderful even if you have just one kind of fruit.

SERVES 2 TO 4

3 lb [1.4 kg] assorted citrus fruits, such as grapefruit, tangerines, and oranges, peeled and sliced into ½-in- [12-cm-] thick rounds.

¼ serrano, thinly sliced (optional)

1 Tbsp honey

1 cup [20 g] packed baby arugula

2 Tbsp chopped fresh mint leaves

1 tsp extra-virgin olive oil

1 tsp white balsamic vinegar or any clear-ish vinegar

⅛ tsp kosher salt

Pinch of freshly ground black pepper

2 Tbsp roughly chopped roasted pistachio nuts

2 oz [55 g] feta cheese, crumbled

On a large platter, arrange the citrus slices flat, mixing up the different colors and sizes as you go. Scatter the serrano around (if using) and drizzle the honey over the citrus.

In a small bowl, toss together the arugula, mint, olive oil, and vinegar. Season with the salt and pepper. Pile the arugula in a tight, high pile atop the citrus slices. Sprinkle the pistachios and feta cheese over the top. Serve immediately.

MAKE AHEAD

Peeling, slicing, and arranging the citrus can be completed several hours in advance. Just wrap your platter in plastic wrap and refrigerate. Don't prepare the arugula until you're ready to eat; it will wilt quickly.

DO YOUR THING

Use avocado slices instead of the feta, and maple syrup instead of the honey to make the recipe vegan. Swap in whatever nuts you have if you don't have pistachios handy.

Rosemary-Gruyère Scones

When I owned a catering company in Coronado, California, I baked scones for the coffee shop next door to my commercial kitchen. I'd bring the imperfect scones home to George—he thought this was the greatest job perk in the world. I still love baking fresh scones for special-occasion mornings like a birthday or an anniversary, and I even let George eat all the perfect ones. These savory scones are just as wonderful for breakfast with scrambled eggs as they are with a warm bowl of soup.

MAKES 8 SCONES

2 cups [280 g] all-purpose flour, plus more for dusting

1 Tbsp sugar

2 tsp baking powder

1¼ tsp kosher salt

1 tsp baking soda

½ tsp freshly ground black pepper

10 Tbsp [140 g] cold unsalted butter, cut into cubes

⅔ cup [160 ml] buttermilk, plus more for brushing

1 cup [60 g] grated Gruyère cheese

2 Tbsp grated Parmesan cheese

2 Tbsp finely chopped fresh rosemary leaves

Pinch of Maldon sea salt

Preheat the oven to 375°F [190°C]. Line a baking sheet with parchment paper.

In a large bowl, whisk the flour, sugar, baking powder, salt, baking soda, and pepper. Toss in the butter cubes and use your fingers to quickly pinch the butter into the flour until the butter pieces are pea size. Add the buttermilk, Gruyère cheese, Parmesan cheese, and rosemary and quickly combine everything with swift hand motions (see Cooking School).

Lightly flour a clean work surface, turn out the dough onto it, and knead it until just combined. It should still look very rough and have visible flecks of butter in it. Use your hands to pat the dough into a 1-in- [2.5-cm-] thick round disk and use a sharp knife to cut across the disk, making 8 triangles.

Transfer the scones to the prepared baking sheet, brush with buttermilk, and sprinkle with the Maldon salt. Bake for 15 to 18 minutes, until golden brown. Allow to cool completely before storing any leftovers in an airtight container for up to 3 days.

MAKE AHEAD

Freeze the uncooked scone dough tightly wrapped in plastic for up to 1 month. Follow the recipe, but bake until golden brown, about 30 minutes.

COOKING SCHOOL

Work quickly with the dough—the colder the butter remains, the flakier your scones will be. That's the true trick to making great biscuits and scones!

Popovers

A popover is part muffin, part pancake, part custard: The top puffs up over the rim of the baking tin cup to become crispy and crunchy, while the bottom bakes into gooey bliss. Popovers look so difficult, but are so easy to make!

Cinnamon Roll Popovers

For those times when only something sweet will do, this cinnamon roll popover recipe delivers on the sticky goodness of a traditional cinnamon roll in a quarter of the time.

MAKES 12 POPOVERS IN A MUFFIN TIN, OR 6 POPOVERS IN A POPOVER TIN

FOR THE CINNAMON ROLL POPOVERS

4 Tbsp [55 g] unsalted butter, melted, plus more for the pan

2 cups [280 g] all-purpose flour

2 cups [480 ml] whole milk

3 large eggs

2 tsp vanilla extract

1 tsp granulated sugar

1 tsp ground cinnamon

½ tsp kosher salt

FOR THE POPOVER GLAZE

1 cup [120 g] powdered sugar

2 Tbsp unsalted butter, at room temperature

2 to 4 Tbsp [30 to 60 ml] boiling water, plus more as needed

Pinch of kosher salt

Preheat the oven to 425°F [220°C]. Butter a 12-cup nonstick muffin tin, or a 6-cup nonstick popover tin.

To make the cinnamon roll popovers: In a blender, combine the flour, milk, eggs, melted butter, vanilla, granulated sugar, cinnamon, and salt. Blend on high speed for 10 seconds. You may need to scrape down the sides of the blender bowl a couple of times.

Fill each muffin cup with batter until just below full. Muffin tins can vary in size, so no worries if you only fill 11, or have a little extra batter. Place the muffin

tin in the middle of the oven and bake for 25 to 30 minutes, until puffed and deep golden brown on top. Keep an eye on them through the door (do not open the door!) starting at the 25-minute mark. If you open the door before they're ready, they'll deflate.

To make the popover glaze: In a small bowl, whisk together the powdered sugar, butter, 2 Tbsp [30 ml] of the boiling water, and salt until smooth. Add more hot water, 1 Tbsp [15 ml] at a time, if needed, to achieve a runny but thick consistency.

Remove the popovers from the oven and immediately pry them out of the tin by sliding a knife around each. Place the popovers on a plate and drizzle with the glaze. Serve immediately!

LEFTOVERS ARE A GOOD THING

Any leftovers can be frozen in an airtight container, once cool, and reheated for 5 to 7 minutes at 350°F [180°C]. Do not put the glaze on if you're going to freeze them.

DO YOUR THING

In a hurry? No need to make the glaze. Sift powdered sugar and cinnamon over the top and serve with melted butter.

COOKING SCHOOL

For brunch parties, pop your filled muffin tin into the oven when the first guest arrives so, by the time you're ready to sit down, your popovers are ready to serve.

Parmesan-Dill Popovers

In addition to being fantastic with a cup of coffee, these savory popovers are also a great substitution for your standard dinner roll. Omit the Parmesan and dill for a classic popover, and serve with butter and jam.

MAKES 12 POPOVERS IN A MUFFIN TIN, OR 6 POPOVERS IN A POPOVER TIN

4 Tbsp [55 g] unsalted butter, melted, plus more for the pan

2 cups [280 g] all-purpose flour

2 cups [480 ml] whole milk

3 large eggs

½ tsp kosher salt

1 cup [30 g] grated Parmesan cheese, plus more for garnishing (optional)

½ cup [5 g] chopped fresh dill, plus more for garnishing (optional)

Preheat the oven to 425°F [220°C]. Butter a 12-cup nonstick muffin tin, or a 6-cup nonstick popover tin.

In a blender, combine the flour, milk, eggs, melted butter, salt, and Parmesan cheese. Blend on high speed for 10 seconds. You may need to scrape down the sides of the blender bowl a couple of times. Add the dill and pulse twice to incorporate into the batter, but do not purée it.

Fill each prepared muffin cup with batter until just below full. Muffin tins can vary in size, so no worries if you only fill 11, or have a little extra batter. Place the muffin tin in the middle of the oven and bake for 25 to 30 minutes, until puffed and deep golden brown

on top. Keep an eye on them through the door (do not open the door!) starting at the 25-minute mark. If you open the door before they're ready, they'll deflate.

Remove the popovers from the oven and immediately pry them from the tin by sliding a knife around each. Place the popovers on a plate and serve immediately! Garnish with an extra sprinkle of chopped dill and Parmesan, if desired.

DO YOUR THING

Swap in whatever hard cheese (Cheddar, Gouda, Pecorino, etc.), and fresh herbs you have on hand. In a pinch, use 1 Tbsp dried herbs in place of fresh herbs.

Sriracha-Maple Breakfast Meatballs

I have to assume you've all experienced the pure ecstasy that occurs when maple syrup drips off your waffle and onto your sausage. These breakfast "meatballs" are that moment reincarnated . . . plus a little Sriracha to spice things up. They also make a dynamite appetizer—serve on a big plate with toothpicks and watch them disappear.

MAKES ABOUT TWENTY-TWO 1-IN [2.5-CM] MEATBALLS

½ cup [30 g] panko bread crumbs

½ tsp kosher salt

¼ tsp red pepper flakes

Pinch of cayenne pepper

1 garlic clove, grated

1 lb [455 g] ground pork

2 Tbsp chopped fresh chives

3 Tbsp maple syrup

2 or 3 Tbsp [30 to 45 ml] Sriracha

Preheat the oven to 400°F [200°C]. Line a baking sheet with parchment paper.

In a large bowl, stir together the bread crumbs, salt, red pepper flakes, cayenne pepper, and garlic. Add the pork, 1 Tbsp of the chives, 2 Tbsp of the maple syrup, and 2 Tbsp of the Sriracha. If you like things very spicy, use 3 Tbsp Sriracha. Use a fork or your clean hands to combine.

Use a tablespoon measuring spoon to scoop meatballs. Place the meatballs on the prepared baking sheet so they do not touch. Bake for 14 minutes.

Meanwhile, in a small bowl, whisk the remaining 1 Tbsp maple syrup with 1 Tbsp Sriracha.

Remove the meatballs from the oven and, while still hot, use a pastry brush to brush the maple syrup-Sriracha glaze over each meatball. Transfer the meatballs from the baking sheet to a serving platter and garnish with the remaining 1 Tbsp chives. Serve immediately.

LEFTOVERS ARE A GOOD THING

This recipe makes a big batch, so freeze leftovers in an airtight container and reheat for 5 to 7 minutes in a 350°F [180°C] oven for breakfast meatballs on the fly.

TOOL TIP

Pastry brushes are a really useful tool. They can be used to brush olive oil evenly over bread slices for toasting, to baste meats during a roast, and to apply glazes, as done here. If you don't have a pastry brush, use a spoon to drizzle a bit of glaze over each meatball. Grate the garlic cloves with a Microplane or on the smallest holes of a box grater.

Breakfast Banh Mi

We once spent ten days in Vietnam and ate banh mi at perhaps every single street stand in Hanoi. We trudged miles across town to try different takes on the sandwich—some with mayo, some overflowing with cilantro, some chicken, some strictly pork. One of our very favorite iterations was an egg banh mi with soft, slow-scrambled eggs. I could never have imagined how wonderful pickled cucumbers and carrots would taste with eggs. We didn't run across any banh mi that included bacon during our time in Vietnam, but it's well worth veering off the path of authenticity for bacon, right?

MAKES 2 SANDWICHES

FOR THE PICKLED CARROTS

6 medium peeled carrots

¼ cup [60 ml] seasoned rice vinegar

2 Tbsp sugar

½ tsp kosher salt

FOR THE BANH MI SANDWICHES

4 bacon slices

Two (10-in [25-cm]) French bread loaves, or 1 baguette, halved widthwise and sliced open horizontally, leaving the back attached

2 Tbsp mayonnaise

2 Tbsp Sriracha

½ jalapeño chile, seeded and thinly sliced

1 cup [20 g] chopped fresh cilantro leaves and stems

1 recipe (use 4 large eggs) Slow-Scrambled Eggs (page 49)

To make the pickled carrots: Use a vegetable peeler to cut the carrots into thin ribbons. Put them into a medium bowl. (If you have a spiralizer, use the flat noodle setting.) Add the vinegar, sugar, and salt and toss to combine. Let sit at room temperature for at least 10 minutes, but preferably for several hours.

To make the banh mi sandwiches: Lay the bacon slices evenly in your largest (cold) nonstick skillet. Place the skillet over medium heat and cook for 4 to 6 minutes per side, until crispy. Transfer to a paper towel-lined plate.

Scoop out a bit of the bread from the bottom half of the baguette pieces to make room for your ingredients. Spread the mayonnaise over the inside top and bottom of the bread. Spread the Sriracha over the mayonnaise. Layer half the jalapeño slices on each, followed by 2 Tbsp drained pickled carrots, 2 bacon slices, and half the cilantro on the bottom half of each sandwich.

Scramble the eggs. Add half to each sandwich. Enjoy immediately.

continued

LEFTOVERS ARE A GOOD THING

Refrigerate extra pickled carrots in an airtight container for up to 1 month and use on sandwiches and salads.

BUY SMART

If you're desperate, buy pre-shredded carrots at the grocery store. They tend to be pretty dried out, so only do this in a pinch.

DO YOUR THING

In place of bacon, try this sandwich with Sriracha-Maple Breakfast Meatballs (page 70) or breakfast sausage links. Not in the mood for scrambled eggs? Try Marbled Eggs (page 49) instead. Make breakfast banh mi tacos by swapping tortillas for baguettes and sour cream for mayonnaise.

Salads AND

Bowl

We often turn to salads and bowls as an option for quick, healthy eating. Sometimes all you need is a really good side salad, which you will find in the Japanese Steakhouse Salad with Miso Ginger Dressing (page 80) and the Shaved Brussels Sprouts Salad (facing page). But other instances call for a bowl full of hearty vegetables, protein, and unbeatable dressings, like the Rainbow Veggie Bowls with Lemon Tahini Dressing (page 88) or the Shrimp Fajita Salad with Avocado Cilantro Dressing (page 92). You will find plenty of options here.

Shaved Brussels Sprouts Salad with Sweet-and-Spicy Nuts and Honey-Mustard Vinaigrette

Some version of deep-fried Brussels sprouts holds a spot on seemingly every restaurant menu right now, but many people don't realize that, when thinly shaved, Brussels sprouts can also be enjoyed raw, like a lettuce green. Marinating them in a whole-grain honey-mustard vinaigrette helps soften the sprouts and infuse them with flavor. A combination of shredded and shaved Parmesan cheese adds texture and salty pops of flavor. George and I especially love to serve this side dish when entertaining during the holidays, since Brussels sprouts are seasonal in winter, and it can be made in advance and served cold or at room temperature.

SERVES 2 AS A MEAL, OR 4 TO 6 AS A SIDE; MAKES ABOUT 1 CUP [140 G] NUTS AND ⅔ CUP [160 ML] VINAIGRETTE

FOR THE SWEET-AND-SPICY NUTS

1 cup toasted, chopped, mixed nuts (I like using pepitas [shelled pumpkin seeds] and walnuts)

¼ cup sugar

1 tablespoon unsalted butter

Pinch of cayenne pepper

Pinch of kosher salt

FOR THE HONEY-MUSTARD VINAIGRETTE

1 large organic lemon

1 Tbsp minced shallot

1 Tbsp whole-grain mustard

1 Tbsp Dijon mustard

2 Tbsp champagne vinegar

2 tsp honey

⅛ tsp kosher salt

⅓ cup [80 ml] extra-virgin olive oil

FOR THE SALAD

12 oz [340 g] fresh Brussels sprouts

4 large (about 4 oz/115 g) Lacinato kale leaves, stemmed

4 dates, pitted and chopped

½ Granny Smith apple or other tart, firm apple, thinly sliced

¼ tsp kosher salt

⅛ tsp freshly cracked black pepper, plus more if needed

1 cup [30 g] finely grated Parmesan cheese

¼ cup [8 g] shaved Parmesan cheese

continued

Preheat the oven to 300°F [150°C] and line a baking sheet with parchment paper.

To make the sweet-and-spicy nuts: Put the nuts, butter, sugar, cayenne pepper, and salt in a medium nonstick skillet over medium heat. Cook, stirring occasionally, until the sugar is melted and the nuts are coated, about 5 minutes. Transfer to a piece of wax paper to cool.

To make the honey-mustard vinaigrette: In a large bowl, zest and juice the lemon. Add the shallot, the whole-grain mustard, the Dijon mustard, the vinegar, honey, and salt. While whisking constantly, slowly drizzle in the olive oil. Set aside.

To make the salad: In a food processor fitted with the blade attachment (or blender), pulse the Brussels sprouts 10 to 15 times, until shredded. Transfer to the bowl with the vinaigrette. Add the kale to the food processor and pulse 4 to 6 times, until shredded. Check on your Brussels sprouts and kale between pulses—you want them shredded, not pulverized into itty-bitty pieces! In the large bowl with the viniagrette, add the kale and the Brussels sprouts, along with the dates, apple, salt, and pepper. Toss thoroughly to coat in dressing. Taste and season with more salt and pepper, if desired. Refrigerate to marinate for at least 15 minutes, but up to 12 hours, before serving.

When ready to eat, toss the grated Parmesan cheese into the salad, transfer the salad to a shallow serving bowl, and garnish with the shaved Parmesan, cheese, a handful of sweet-and-spicy nuts, and more pepper, if desired.

LEFTOVERS ARE A GOOD THING

You'll have leftover nuts. Sprinkle them over ice cream for a sweet and spicy crunch, toss into any salad or bowl, or serve them to guests as a cocktail nut.

DO YOUR THING

Not into Brussels sprouts? Make the entire salad with kale. Maybe throw some shredded cabbage in there. Marinated salads such as this one do best with tough, chewy greens such as kale and cabbage.

Japanese Steakhouse Salad with Miso Ginger Dressing

One of the guilty pleasures I share with George is cheap Japanese food (preferably found in a nondescript strip mall in the Southeast). Teriyaki steak over steamed white rice? Sign us up! We both love the carrot-y, ginger-y dressing that comes with the often included salad, but the limp iceberg lettuce and mealy, underripe tomatoes don't exactly do it for us. I started making the dressing at home, and even with just the two of us, this large batch disappears in days.

SERVES 2 TO 4

1 head Bibb lettuce, torn into bite-size pieces

¼ cup [30 g] julienned radishes

1 Persian cucumber, or ½ English cucumber, thinly sliced

½ cup [120 ml] Miso Ginger Dressing (recipe follows)

1 avocado, cut into ¼-in- [6-mm-] thick slices

2 Tbsp Pickled Red Onions (page 82)

1 tsp sesame seeds, toasted

In a large bowl, toss the lettuce, radishes, and cucumber with the dressing. Transfer to a shallow serving bowl and scatter the avocado, red onions, and sesame seeds over the top.

MAKE AHEAD

Make the dressing and chop your veggies up to 24 hours in advance, but don't toss this salad until the very last minute. The dressing is really heavy and the salad will become soggy if not eaten immediately.

DO YOUR THING

A traditional Japanese steakhouse salad consists of iceberg lettuce, chopped tomatoes, and sliced cucumber. I don't like tomatoes with this dressing, so I omit them.

Miso Ginger Dressing

MAKES 2 CUPS [480 ML]

4 medium carrots, peeled and roughly chopped

One (2-in [2.5-cm]) piece peeled fresh ginger, roughly chopped

⅓ cup [80 ml] rice vinegar

⅓ cup [80 ml] grapeseed oil or other neutral oil

¼ cup [60 ml] water

2 Tbsp toasted sesame oil

2 Tbsp white miso paste

2 tsp honey

¼ tsp kosher salt

¼ tsp freshly ground black pepper

In a blender, combine the carrots, ginger, vinegar, grapeseed oil, water, sesame oil, miso, honey, salt, and pepper. Blend on high speed for 30 seconds, or until smooth. Refrigerate in an airtight container for up to 1 week.

DO YOUR THING

I once tasked George with making this dressing when we were cooking dinner for a few couples. He "accidentally" (read: too lazy to go to the grocery store) used tahini in place of miso paste, and everyone (myself included) *absolutely loved it*. His cooking ego tripled that night, and he still claims "his" *Tahini* Ginger Dressing is the best (wink: only) recipe he's ever written.

COOKING SCHOOL

The easiest way to peel ginger is not with a vegetable peeler, but by using the dull edge of a spoon to gently scrape off the skin.

Pickled Red Onions

We keep a jar of these in our refrigerator at all times to keep meals interesting. They make the perfect finishing garnish, providing crunchy acidic punch atop Juiciest Pork Tenderloin (page 184), on any salad, in tacos, and over Sautéed Spinach with Baked Eggs and Feta (page 58).

MAKES ABOUT 1½ CUPS [360 G]

1 large red onion, halved and sliced into half-moons

2 garlic cloves, crushed

1 Tbsp sugar

1 tsp kosher salt

½ cup [120 ml] red wine vinegar

½ cup [120 ml] water

In an airtight sealable container, combine the onion, garlic, sugar, salt, vinegar, and water. Cover and shake for about 15 seconds to combine. Let sit for 30 minutes to 1 hour at room temperature. Enjoy or refrigerate for up to 2 weeks.

DO YOUR THING

Add seeded and minced jalapeño or habanero chile for spicy pickled onions, just like the ones you find at taco stands all over Mexico.

COOKING SCHOOL

Once you get hooked on this recipe, try different onions (I like white onions and shallots) with different vinegars for a variety of pickled onions.

Crunchy-Tangy Vietnamese Chicken Salad

While in Vietnam, George and I went on an overnight boat cruise in Halong Bay. Both of us secretly expected to hate it (we are pretty cruise ship–averse), but our worries quickly faded when we sat down for lunch the first day and were greeted by the most beautiful lunch that included fresh seafood and this crunchy, tangy, salty, slaw-ish salad.

SERVES 2

1 lb [455 g] boneless, skinless chicken breasts

1 Tbsp kosher salt

1 recipe Tangy Vietnamese Dressing (page 84)

2 cups [120 g] packed shredded napa cabbage

1 cup [60 g] packed shredded red cabbage

1 bunch fresh cilantro leaves and stems, chopped (about 1 cup [40 g])

1 bunch fresh mint leaves, chopped (about ½ cup [20 g])

½ English cucumber, thinly sliced

1 Thai red chile, seeded and thinly sliced

4 scallions, light green and white parts only, thinly sliced

2 Tbsp toasted sesame seeds

¼ cup [35 g] chopped roasted salted peanuts

In the bottom of a medium saucepan, arrange the chicken in a single layer. Sprinkle with the salt and cover with 1 in [2.5 cm] of water. Bring the water to a boil over high heat, turn the heat to low, and cover the pot. Simmer for 10 to 14 minutes, until an instant-read thermometer registers an internal temperature in the chicken of 165°F [75°C]. Drain and place the chicken on a cutting board.

Pour the dressing into a large bowl. When the chicken is cool enough to handle, use your hands to shred it into strips into the bowl with the dressing. Toss to coat and set aside for several minutes to soak up the dressing.

Add the napa and red cabbage, cilantro, mint, cucumber, chile, scallions, and sesame seeds. Toss to combine and let sit for several minutes to marinate before serving. Sprinkle the peanuts on at the last minute, because they get soggy if tossed in too early.

LEFTOVERS ARE A GOOD THING

After a night in the fridge, the cabbage softens a bit, and this salad becomes more of a Vietnamese chicken slaw. It's delicious!

MAKE IT A MEAL

Skip the chicken, and instead serve this salad alongside Pan-Seared Scallops with Strawberry-Avocado Salsa (page 167), Fig-Glazed Pork Belly (page 183), or Vietnamese Chicken Skewers with Grilled Scalliions (page 195).

Tangy Vietnamese Dressing

MAKES ABOUT 1 CUP (240 ML)

3 Tbsp fish sauce

3 Tbsp fresh lime juice (from about 2 limes)

2 Tbsp rice vinegar

2 Tbsp water

2 Tbsp grapeseed oil or other neutral oil

2 Tbsp sesame oil

1 Tbsp sugar

2 garlic cloves, grated

2 tsp sambal oelek

In a large bowl, whisk together the fish sauce, lime juice, vinegar, water, grapeseed oil, toasted sesame oil, sugar, garlic, and sambal oelek until combined. Transfer to an airtight container. Keep refrigerated and use within 10 days.

SPECIAL INGREDIENT

Don't be put off by the undeniably funky smell of fish sauce. It's crucial to creating certain authentic Asian flavors at home. It's great as a marinade: Try marinating a couple pounds of chicken in a mixture of 3 Tbsp fish sauce, ½ cup [120 ml] soy sauce, ¼ cup [60 ml] fresh orange juice, 2 Tbsp sesame oil, and 3 or 4 minced garlic cloves overnight before grilling it.

DO YOUR THING

Whisk in 1 or 2 Tbsp of smooth peanut butter for a Vietnamese peanut dressing.

Miso-Glazed Carrot and Radish Quinoa Bowls

George and I are both Southerners, so we both grew up eating honey-glazed carrots as a regular side dish. Adding miso and radishes to the mix makes this dish feel grown up and gourmet, but it's really just as easy as boiling carrots!

SERVES 2

FOR THE MISO QUINOA

1¼ cups [300 ml] water

1 tsp miso paste

1 cup [180 g] dry uncooked quinoa, rinsed well

FOR THE BOWL

Juice of 1 lemon

2 Tbsp unsalted butter

1 Tbsp miso paste

1 tsp maple syrup

1½ cups [360 ml] water, plus more as needed

2 bunches carrots (about 12 oz [340 g]), washed and trimmed

1 bunch small radishes (about 4 oz [115 g]), washed and halved

1 cup [20 g] baby greens (kale, arugula, spring greens)

1 small avocado, thinly sliced

4 Tbsp [90 g] Garlicky Quinoa Crispies (page 87)

½ lemon, cut into wedges

To make the miso quinoa: In a small pot over high heat, whisk the water and miso paste. Stir in the quinoa, bring to a boil, cover the pot, and turn the heat to low. Simmer for 15 minutes. Remove from the heat and let sit, covered, for at least 10 minutes. Fluff with a fork.

To make the bowl contents: In a large skillet or saucepan over high heat, combine the lemon juice, butter, miso paste, maple syrup, and water. Whisk until the butter melts and all ingredients are well combined.

Add the carrots and radishes, arranged so they are all covered with liquid. If needed, add a bit more water. Lower the heat to medium-high and cook for 15 minutes, or until the vegetables are fork-tender, stirring a couple of times. If the liquid evaporates before the vegetables are tender, add 1 Tbsp of water at a time until they are cooked. When the liquid evaporates and only a sticky glaze remains, remove the skillet from the heat and stir the vegetables to coat completely in the glaze.

Divide the miso quinoa and baby greens between two shallow bowls. Arrange the glazed vegetables, avocado slices, and 2 Tbsp of Garlicky Quinoa Crispies over the top. Serve with a fresh lemon wedge.

continued

Not a fan of radishes? Try another root vegetable, such as turnips, beets, fennel, or parsnips. Or, stick to all carrots. Too healthy-sounding for your vegetable-averse partner? Add their favorite cheese! Goat cheese and feta work beautifully here.

Most quinoa packages call for a 1 cup quinoa [180 g] to 2 cups [480 ml] water ratio, which I find leads to soggy, wet quinoa. I always cook mine with a ratio of 1 cup [180 g] quinoa to 1¼ cups [300 ml] water, as seen here.

BACK POCKET RECIPE

Garlicky Quinoa Crispies

I like to whip up a batch of these crispy little superfood crouton stand-ins to make texture-filled salads, bowls, and veggie dishes to enjoy throughout the week. Try them in place of bread crumbs over Roasted Cabbage with Brown Butter Bread Crumbs (page 231), or forego the garlic powder and red pepper flakes to sprinkle them over fruit and yogurt as an alternative to granola.

MAKES 2 CUPS [740 G]

Vegetable oil for frying

2 cups [740 g] cooked quinoa

½ tsp garlic powder

¼ tsp kosher salt

Pinch of red pepper flakes

In a large skillet over medium-high heat, heat ½ in [12 mm] vegetable oil. Working in ¼-cup [92.5-g] batches, fry the quinoa for 1½ to 2 minutes until dark brown and crispy. Use a spider skimmer or slotted spoon to transfer the quinoa to a paper towel-lined plate to drain. Once it is all cooked, drained, and cooled slightly, transfer the quinoa to an airtight container, add the garlic powder, salt, and red pepper flakes. Cover and shake to combine. Store in the airtight container at room temperature for up to 10 days.

Rainbow Veggie Bowls with Lemon Tahini Dressing

I don't know what my favorite part of this recipe is: how easy cleanup is or how delicious the Lemon Tahini Dressing tastes drizzled over the caramelized, roasted vegetables. Grab two aprons and head into the kitchen together—there's a lot to chop, and there's no such thing as too many cooks in the kitchen when you're there with your love! The portion here is big, because when we eat a bowl of veggies as our meal, we like to eat a lot of them!

SERVES 2

1 large (12-oz [340-g]) sweet potato, peeled and cut into ½-in [1-cm] cubes

1 medium beet (8 oz [230 g]), peeled and cut into ½-in [1-cm] cubes

8 oz [230 g] cremini mushrooms, halved

1 large fennel bulb, trimmed and cut into ¼-in-by-1-in [6-mm-by-2.5-cm] slices

1 Tbsp olive oil

¼ tsp kosher salt

¼ tsp garlic powder

⅛ tsp freshly ground black pepper

½ cup [90 g] uncooked wild or brown rice

1 cup [20 g] packed fresh baby spinach

1 recipe Lemon Tahini Dressing (recipe follows)

Preheat the oven to 425°F [220°C]. Line a large baking sheet with aluminum foil.

On the prepared baking sheet, arrange the sweet potato, beet, mushrooms, and fennel in rows. Drizzle with the olive oil and season with the salt, garlic powder, and pepper. Toss gently but maintain the separate rows. Spread the vegetables so they touch as little as possible. Roast for 20 to 25 minutes, or until the sweet potato is easily pierced with a fork. The beets will maintain a bit of a bite—if you like them softer, remove all other vegetables from the baking sheet and cook the beets for 10 minutes more.

Meanwhile, cook the rice (see Quick Cooking Reference Guide, page 263).

Divide the cooked rice and baby spinach between two bowls and top with your desired amount of roasted vegetables. Drizzle with the dressing and enjoy!

MAKE AHEAD

This is a great technique for meal prep! Double or triple the recipe and keep the veggies in separate airtight containers so you can mix and match, and make your own bowls and salads all week long.

DO YOUR THING

Swap in your favorite vegetables and just keep an eye on them in the oven, because they may cook faster or slower than the veggies in this recipe.

Lemon Tahini Dressing

George and I spent a week in Tel Aviv, Israel, last year and I can say without hesitation that we enjoyed the best food we've ever eaten. Every meal was meticulously planned to ensure we tasted all the Israeli specialties I'd read about beforehand: freshly made hummus, hummshuka (shakshuka baked over hummus!), sabich (fried eggplant pita sandwich), and the list goes on and on. I already loved tahini—a paste made from ground sesame seeds—but tasting it freshly ground, straight from the source gave me an entirely new respect for it. It's now my secret weapon for creating thick, creamy, flavorful sauces and dressings.

MAKES ABOUT 1 CUP (ABOUT 240 G)

¼ cup [55 g] tahini

⅓ cup [80 ml] warm water

¼ cup [60 g] plain yogurt

1 tsp maple syrup or honey

Juice of 1 lemon

1 garlic clove, grated

¼ tsp kosher salt

Freshly ground black pepper

In a large bowl, whisk together the tahini, water, yogurt, maple syrup, lemon juice, garlic, and the salt, and season with black pepper. Depending on the thickness of your tahini, you may need to whisk in 1 Tbsp warm water at a time until you reach the desired consistency. Refrigerate in an airtight container for up to 3 days.

SPECIAL INGREDIENT

For a sweet application, try tahini in place of almond butter in the Almond-Banana Smoothie (page 28) or Coronado Cookies (page 240), or add a scoop of it to the California Date Shake (page 262).

BUY SMART

Look for tahini that is smooth and doesn't separate (oil on top, solids on the bottom). Thrive Market and Trader Joe's both sell affordable, high-quality products.

DO YOUR THING

This dressing is just as great dairy-free—simply omit the yogurt and sub in a couple tablespoons of extra-virgin olive oil.

Farmers' Market Salad with Apple Cider Vinaigrette

This salad celebrates the seasons and the opportunity to come together over a simple and restorative meal. Use this recipe as a basic outline to create a salad from your own seasonal farmers' market bounty. The sweetness from the grapes and dates, salt from the feta, creaminess from the avocado, and crunch from the almonds all work so well together but can easily be swapped for what's available at your market (or in the back of your fridge).

SERVES 2 AS A MEAL

1 bunch (about 1 lb [455 g]) fresh kale, stemmed and cut into ¼-in- [6-mm-] thick ribbons

Pinch of kosher salt

3 Tbsp Apple Cider Vinaigrette (recipe follows)

1 tsp grapeseed oil

½ cup [70 g] fresh corn kernels

½ cup [80 g] red grapes, halved

2 dates, pitted and chopped

¼ lb [115 g] sliced turkey, cut into ¼-in- [6-mm-] thick strips

2 oz [55 g] feta cheese, crumbled, or Fried Goat Cheese (page 215)

1 small avocado, sliced

2 Tbsp toasted almonds, chopped

⅛ tsp Maldon sea salt

Freshly ground black pepper

Wash and dry the kale thoroughly and transfer to a large bowl. Sprinkle with the kosher salt and use your hands to "massage" it by scrunching it up in your fists over and over until it begins to break down and release its juices, 15 to 30 seconds. Toss with the vinaigrette, transfer to a shallow serving bowl, and set aside.

In a small skillet over medium-high heat, warm the grapeseed oil. Add the corn and cook for 2 to 4 minutes until blistered and cooked through. Transfer to the bowl with the kale, and add the grapes and dates. Toss to combine.

Divide the salad between two bowls and top with half of the turkey, feta, avocado, and almonds. Season with the sea salt and pepper.

SEASONALITY

This salad is all about celebrating whatever's in season. Try peaches instead of grapes, goat cheese instead of feta, and add Pickled Red Onions (page 82) for a winning summer salad.

MAKE IT A MEAL

To make this salad more of a dinner than lunch dish, replace the turkey with a couple of Yogurt-Marinated Chicken Skewers with Yogurt Sauce (page 194).

Apple Cider Vinaigrette

This classic vinaigrette is made distinctly autumnal with apple cider vinegar and maple syrup.

MAKES ABOUT ¾ CUP [180 ML] DRESSING

½ cup [120 ml] apple cider vinegar

1 Tbsp minced shallot

1 Tbsp Dijon mustard

1 tsp maple syrup or honey

Pinch of kosher salt

Pinch of freshly ground black pepper

¼ cup [60 ml] extra-virgin olive oil

In a small bowl, stir together the vinegar, shallot, mustard, maple syrup, salt, and pepper. While whisking, slowly pour in the olive oil to emulsify. Refrigerate in an airtight glass container for up to 1 week.

DO YOUR THING

Use whatever sweetener or vinegar you have on hand, and add flavor with your favorite spices such as paprika or coriander.

SPECIAL INGREDIENT

Apple cider vinegar is a really versatile ingredient that can be used in a number of applications outside of the kitchen. Mix a tablespoon into your tea if you're dealing with an upset stomach; it helps aid digestion.

Shrimp Fajita Salad with Avocado Cilantro Dressing

This recipe is a two-for-one: a quick, tasty shrimp fajita recipe, plus a recipe for how to turn those fajitas into a delicious salad with creamy avocado cilantro dressing. If you're looking for a vegetarian option, the salad holds up perfectly well on its own without the shrimp.

SERVES 2

1 tsp chili powder

½ tsp garlic powder

½ tsp kosher salt

Pinch of cayenne pepper

1 lb [455 g] shrimp, peeled and deveined

1 Tbsp grapeseed oil

1 red bell pepper, seeded and cut into ⅛-in [4-mm] strips

½ yellow onion, cut into ⅛-in [4-mm] half-moons

3 cups [80 g] packed chopped romaine lettuce

1 cup [20 g] packed chopped kale

½ cup [60 g] julienned jicama

½ cup [20 g] fresh cilantro leaves, roughly chopped

2 Tbsp Avocado Cilantro Dressing (page 94)

1 small mango, cubed

1 small avocado, thinly sliced

In a large bowl, mix together the chili powder, garlic powder, salt, and cayenne pepper. Add the shrimp and toss to coat.

In a large nonstick skillet over medium-high heat, heat the grapeseed oil. Add the red bell pepper and onion and cook for 4 to 5 minutes, until they begin to soften. Add the shrimp and cook for 3 minutes more, stirring until cooked through (they should look pink and opaque). Set aside.

In another large bowl, toss together the romaine lettuce, kale, jicama, cilantro, and dressing. Divide the salad between two serving bowls. Top with the shrimp mixture, mango, and avocado.

MAKE IT A MEAL

Forget salads; make it fajita night! Cook just the shrimp fajita mixture and serve with corn tortillas, fresh cilantro, shredded cheese, sour cream, and salsa.

BUY SMART

Jicama can be difficult to find in its root form, but most major grocery stores now carry it in their prepared section, pre-cut! If you can find it in root form, I like to peel it and spiralize it to take all the work out of chopping, and add a fun texture to this salad.

Avocado Cilantro Dressing

This dressing will satisfy your craving for a creamy, decadent salad dressing without all the unhealthy fat of a Caesar or traditional green goddess dressing. What's life without a little decadence?

MAKES ABOUT 1¼ CUPS [300 ML]

1 small avocado or ½ large avocado	½ tsp salt
1 cup [20 g] fresh cilantro leaves and stems	¼ tsp freshly ground black pepper
½ cup [120 ml] water	¼ tsp red pepper flakes
⅓ cup [80 g] plain yogurt	Juice of 2 limes
1 large garlic clove	½ fresh jalapeño chile, seeded (optional)

In a food processor or blender, combine the avocado, cilantro, water, yogurt, garlic, salt, black pepper, red pepper flakes, lime juice, and the jalapeño chile, if using, for a little heat, and blend until smooth. If the dressing is too thick, add 1 Tbsp of water at a time until you have the desired consistency, which is about the consistency of Caesar salad dressing.

DO YOUR THING

Use olive oil instead of yogurt to make this dressing dairy-free. Basil is a great substitute for the cilantro. Or, use a mixture of cilantro, basil, and parsley to make your own version of a green goddess dressing.

COOKING SCHOOL

There's a right way and a wrong way to cut an avocado. The wrong way often results in sliced hands and fingers. Using a chef's knife, slice down from the stem end until you feel the pit. Rotate the avocado around the blade until the two cuts meet. Set your knife aside. Twist the avocado halves in separate directions until they pull apart. To remove the pit, firmly whack the base of your knife into the pit, then twist until the pit loosens and you can remove it. Scoop the flesh out with a large spoon.

Soups

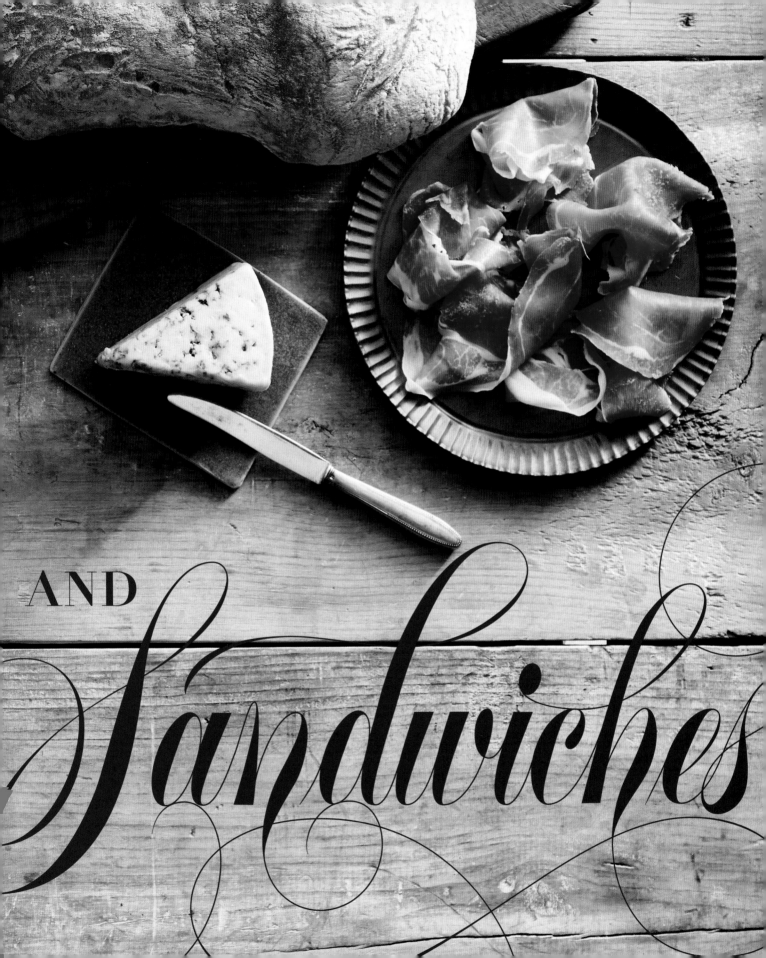

AND

Sandwiches

Soups and sandwiches equal total comfort food. When we're chilled to the bone on a cold winter day, we warm up with a big bowl of creamy hot soup, like Chipotle Butternut Squash Soup with Crunchy Croutons (page 104). Starving after a long hike with friends? Good thing you packed Pressed Focaccia Sandwiches (page 106)! This chapter arms you with a new collection of craveable soup and sandwich recipes for any occasion.

Gazpacho with Charred Jalapeño Crema

Growing up in North Carolina, we'd make gazpacho by the gallon and eat it for breakfast, lunch, and dinner on hot summer days. I've upgraded my gazpacho a bit since then, swapping in fresh tomatoes for Clamato juice and adding a charred jalapeño crema. This gazpacho is one of George and my go-tos for impromptu summer celebrations—almost all the work is done in a blender, so even the novice cook can lend a hand.

SERVES 4 TO 6; MAKES ABOUT ½ CUP [120 G] CREMA

FOR THE GAZPACHO

3 red bell peppers, halved and seeded

2 (about ¾ lb [340 g] each) English cucumbers, peeled

1½ lb [680 g] ripe Roma tomatoes, roughly chopped

½ jalapeño chile, seeded and roughly chopped (reserve the other half for the jalapeño crema)

¼ yellow onion, roughly chopped

¼ cup [60 ml] sherry vinegar

¾ tsp kosher salt

½ tsp freshly ground black pepper

2 Tbsp extra-virgin olive oil

FOR THE CHARRED JALAPEÑO CREMA

½ jalapeño chile, seeded

½ cup [120 g] Greek yogurt

1 tsp fresh lemon juice

Pinch of salt

To make the gazpacho: Roughly chop 1 red bell pepper and 1 cucumber and put into the blender. Add the tomatoes, jalapeño chile, onion, vinegar, salt, and black pepper. Blend for 45 seconds to 1 minute on high speed, until completely smooth. Turn the blender to low speed and slowly drizzle in the olive oil until combined, about 15 seconds. Pour into a large bowl. (Some people prefer to strain their gazpacho base through a fine-mesh sieve for a smooth consistency. I am not one of those people—I like texture! If you are, do that now.)

Finely dice the remaining 2 red bell peppers and 1 cucumber. Stir them into the purée. Taste and season with additional vinegar, salt, and black pepper, if needed. Cover the bowl with plastic wrap and refrigerate overnight, or for at least 5 hours before serving so the flavors can blend.

To make the charred jalapeño crema: If you have a gas stove, turn a burner onto the highest setting. Using tongs, hold the jalapeño half directly in the flame until it is charred all over. If you have an electric stove, place the jalapeño half under the broiler until

continued

charred all over, turning every 4 minutes or so. Transfer to the blender.

In the blender, add the yogurt, lemon juice, and salt. Blend for 10 to 15 seconds, until smooth. Transfer to an airtight container and refrigerate until ready to use. It will keep for up to 5 days.

To serve, transfer the soup to bowls and serve with a dollop of the jalapeño crema.

TOOL TIP

Mini food processors are great for blending or chopping small quantities, like a handful of nuts, or this crema. You can use your regular blender, but you may have to scrape down the sides several times to make sure everything blends properly.

DO YOUR THING

Too hot to turn on the stove? Forget the Charred Jalapeño Crema and serve your gazpacho with a dollop of chilled sour cream like we did when I was growing up. It's not fancy, but it sure is good.

Creamy Miso Mushroom Soup

This soup gets its luscious creaminess from coconut milk, and its unique salty, savory flavor from a hearty dose of miso. It may sound exotic, but even the least adventurous eaters will love this soup. It's like your classic cream of mushroom soup, brought into this decade.

MAKES ABOUT 5 CUPS [1.2 L]

1 Tbsp unsalted butter

2 celery stalks, diced

2 medium carrots, diced

1 large shallot, diced

2 garlic cloves, minced

12 oz [340 g] cremini mushrooms, chopped

2 to 2½ cups [480 to 600 ml] chicken broth, plus more as needed

One 13.5-fl oz [400-ml] can unsweetened coconut milk

3 Tbsp white miso paste

Kosher salt

Freshly cracked black pepper

Finely chopped fresh parsley leaves for topping (optional)

Freshly grated Parmesan cheese for topping (optional)

In a large heavy-bottomed pot (like a Dutch oven) over medium-low heat, combine the butter, celery, carrots, shallot, and garlic. Cook for about 5 minutes, stirring frequently, until the vegetables are soft and the shallot is translucent. If the vegetables start to brown, turn the heat down.

Add the mushrooms and cook for 6 to 10 minutes more, or until the mushrooms release their juices and the juices have cooked off. When you first add the mushrooms, you may need to add a splash of broth if the pot seems dry.

Stir in 2 cups [480 ml] of the broth and the coconut milk. Raise the heat to high to bring the soup to a boil. Turn the heat to medium-low, stir in the miso, and simmer for 15 minutes.

Turn off the heat and let the soup cool for at least 10 minutes before transferring it to a high-powered blender. It is very important to let the soup cool. If you blend a hot substance on high speed, the pressure will blow the lid off your blender, the soup will go flying, and you'll probably get some gnarly burns. Patience! Blend the soup for 1 minute on high speed.

Taste the soup for two things: consistency and saltiness. I like this soup very thick, like a bisque, but if you want to thin it a bit, add ¼ cup [60 ml] broth, blend, and taste it again. Blend in more broth until you've reached the desired consistency. Your miso may be salty enough so you don't need to add any salt—taste to decide. Add a few grinds of fresh pepper, blend for a couple of seconds, and pour the soup back into the pot.

When you're ready to eat, reheat the soup gently over medium-low heat with the lid on. Ladle into bowls and finish with a sprinkle of parsley and a shower of freshly grated Parmesan cheese, if desired, and freshly cracked black pepper.

DO YOUR THING

Make the soup vegan by swapping 1 Tbsp of olive oil for the butter, 2 cups [480 ml] vegetable broth for the chicken broth, and foregoing the Parmesan cheese.

COOKING SCHOOL

Mirepoix (pronounced *meer-pwah*) is called the "holy trinity" in the cooking world. This triple threat of yellow onion, carrot, and celery adds aroma and flavor to dishes from soups to braises to stocks. I don't provide precise measurements here (i.e., 1 cup [120 g] diced celery) because it just doesn't matter. You can always sub leeks or shallots (as I did) for the onion, parsnips for the carrots, and celery root or fennel for the celery. Most major grocery stores sell pre-diced mirepoix and sliced mushrooms in the refrigerated section. Go for it. Use 1½ cups [180 g] mirepoix.

BUY SMART

Canned "lite coconut milk" is just diluted coconut milk. It's about 50 percent water, 50 percent coconut milk, for the same price as a can of 100 percent coconut milk! If you want to lighten a recipe that calls for a can of coconut milk, use a half can of full-fat coconut milk and a half can of water. Save the remaining coconut milk for another use.

Chipotle Butternut Squash Soup with Crunchy Croutons

This creamy soup is just what the doctor ordered on a chilly fall or winter day. I love making a big batch on Sunday so we can enjoy it all week long. The sweet and spicy croutons are seriously addictive and worth the extra effort.

SERVES 6 TO 8

FOR THE SOUP

2 Tbsp unsalted butter

1 small yellow onion, diced

3 garlic cloves, chopped

½ tsp ground cumin

½ tsp ground cinnamon

1 tsp kosher salt

3 lb [1.4 kg] butternut squash, peeled and cubed

1 qt [960 ml] chicken broth

1 canned chipotle chile in adobo sauce, halved and seeds scraped out

½ cup [120 g] heavy cream

Juice of 1 large orange (about ¼ cup [60 ml])

FOR THE CRUNCHY CROUTONS

2 Tbsp unsalted butter, melted

¼ tsp kosher salt

½ tsp adobo sauce (sauce from canned chipotle chiles)

1 tsp sugar

2 cups [about 60 g] 1-in [2.5 cm] cubed day-old bread

Mexican crema or sour cream for topping (optional)

To make the soup: In a large pot over medium heat, melt the butter. Add the onion, garlic, cumin, cinnamon, and salt. Cook for 4 minutes, until the onion is translucent. Add the squash, chicken broth, and chipotle chile. Raise the heat to high to bring the soup to a boil. Turn the heat to low and simmer for 30 to 40 minutes, or until the squash is very tender. Stir in the heavy cream. Remove from the heat.

Preheat the oven to 400°F [200°C].

To make the crunchy croutons: In a large bowl, stir together the melted butter, salt, adobo sauce, and sugar. Add the bread and toss to coat evenly in the butter mixture. Spread the bread cubes evenly on a baking sheet and bake for 10 to 12 minutes, until golden brown. Set aside to cool.

Let the soup cool for at least 10 minutes before transferring it to a high-power blender. It is very important to let the soup cool. If you blend a hot substance on high speed, the pressure will blow the lid off the blender, the soup will go flying, and you'll probably get some gnarly burns. Patience! Blend in batches for 1 minute on high speed. Return the soup to the pot, stir in the orange juice, and taste for seasoning. If you'd like it spicier, stir in some of the adobo sauce from the chipotle can.

Ladle the soup into bowls, swirl in the Mexican crema or sour cream, if desired, top with the croutons, and serve immediately.

SPECIAL INGREDIENT

Chipotles in adobo are a super flavorful ingredient. After you open the can, transfer them to an airtight glass container and they'll keep in the refrigerator for months. Try swapping chipotle in for the harissa in the Harissa Braised Short Ribs (page 205).

DO YOUR THING

For a classic butternut squash soup, eliminate the chipotle and orange juice. To make this dairy free, use ½ cup coconut milk in place of the heavy cream.

BUY SMART

Almost all major grocery stores now sell pre-cut butternut squash. Save yourself the hassle of tackling a butternut squash!

Pressed Focaccia Sandwiches

George and I love taking our dog, Hooper, on long hikes on the weekend. It's really fun to pack a simple picnic that can be thrown into a backpack and enjoyed from a beautiful vista. Pressed focaccia sandwiches are the perfect picnic food because they are compressed and won't fall apart when they jostle around a picnic basket or backpack. Portioned into small bite-size squares, they also make a perfect finger food for a luncheon.

Gochujang Chicken Salad Sandwiches

Classic chicken salad with grapes and celery is deliciously comforting, but sometimes something new and exciting is called for. Gochujang is a Korean chile paste with a subtle sweetness and mild spice, and turns what is typically a pretty underwhelming dish—chicken salad—into something with a lot of depth.

SERVES 2 TO 4

FOR THE GOCHUJANG CHICKEN SALAD

2 lb [910 g] bone-in, skin-on chicken breasts (2 to 4 breasts, depending on size)

¾ tsp kosher salt

½ tsp freshly ground black pepper

2 Tbsp olive oil

½ cup [70 g] thinly sliced scallions

FOR THE DRESSING

⅓ cup [80 g] mayonnaise

2 Tbsp gochujang

1 Tbsp rice vinegar

1 Tbsp sesame oil

FOR THE CHICKEN SALAD SANDWICHES

½ focaccia loaf

3 Tbsp mayonnaise (optional)

2 cups [40 g] mixed greens

¼ cup [35 g] thinly sliced radishes

½ cup [65 g] thinly sliced cucumber

1 cup [20 g] fresh cilantro, stems trimmed to 1 in [2.5 cm]

Preheat the oven to 400°F [200°C].

To make the gochujang chicken salad: Place the chicken breasts on a baking sheet and sprinkle with salt and pepper. Rub with olive oil. Roast for 40 to 45 minutes, or until the chicken registers an internal temperature of 165°F [75°C]. Remove from the oven and let cool.

While the chicken roasts, make the dressing: In a small bowl, whisk the mayonnaise, gochujang, rice vinegar, and sesame oil.

When the chicken is cool, pull off the skin and pull the meat off the bones. Discard the skin and bones (or reserve to make No-Recipe Bone Broth, page 263). Pull the chicken into small strips and place in a large bowl. Add half the dressing to the chicken, stir to combine, and slowly add more dressing until it's to your liking. (I like my chicken salad really moist, so I use the entire amount. Some like it more on the dry side. As always, do your thing.) Stir in the scallions, cover, and refrigerate until ready to use.

To assemble the sandwiches: Slice the focaccia bread in half horizontally, so you have an equal-size top and bottom. Spread mayonnaise, if using, over the cut side of both bread halves. Spread the mixed greens over the bottom half of the bread and layer the radishes, 1 cup of the chicken salad, cucumber, and cilantro over the top.

Place the top half of the bread on the sandwich and press down lightly. Place a plate on top of the sandwich and weigh it down with several heavy objects (such as books) for 10 to 15 minutes. Slice into four squares and enjoy immediately or wrap tightly in plastic wrap to enjoy later.

SPECIAL INGREDIENT

Gochujang is a flavor-packed chili paste that I also use in Korean Sliced Beef (page 182) and that would make a great substitute for harissa in Harissa Braised Short Ribs (page 205).

DO YOUR THING

Replace the gochujang with Sriracha, curry paste, or buffalo wing sauce for a different spin on this spicy chicken salad.

COOKING SCHOOL

Spreading mayonnaise on the top and bottom of the bread halves helps the sandwich hold together, but since you've already used a lot of mayonnaise in the chicken salad, I list it as optional for assembling the sandwiches.

Grilled Vegetable and Prosciutto Sandwiches

Cured meats and vegetables are ideal for picnicking since they are easy to transport and won't spoil if they sit out all day, and I love the way this pressed sandwich cuts up neatly into uniform little squares with perfect layers for easy eating.

SERVES 2 TO 4

8 oz [230 g] yellow squash, cut lengthwise into ¼-in- [6-mm-] thick planks

8 oz [230 g] zucchini, cut lengthwise into ¼-in- [6-mm-] thick planks

1 large (about 12 oz [340 g]) Chinese eggplant, cut lengthwise into ¼-in- [6-mm-] thick planks

2 Tbsp olive oil

½ tsp garlic powder

¼ tsp kosher salt

¼ tsp freshly ground black pepper

½ focaccia loaf

3 Tbsp Artichoke Tapenade (facing page)

2 oz [55 g] goat cheese

4 oz [115 g] thinly sliced prosciutto

4 oz [115 g] fresh mozzarella cheese, cut into ¼-in [6-mm] slices

2 cups [40 g] fresh baby spinach

Preheat a grill, or a grill pan, to medium-high heat.

Place the squash, zucchini, and eggplant on a large baking sheet, drizzle with olive oil, and sprinkle with the garlic powder, salt, and pepper. Toss to coat. Grill the vegetables for about 8 minutes per side, until dark grill marks appear and the vegetables are very tender. Transfer back to the baking sheet in a single layer and set aside to cool.

Slice the focaccia in half horizontally, so you have an equal-size top and bottom. Spread artichoke tapenade on the cut side of the bottom half of the bread. Spread goat cheese on the cut side of the top half of the bread. Starting on the bottom half, layer the prosciutto, squash, zucchini, mozzarella, eggplant, and spinach. Place the top half of the bread on the sandwich and press down lightly. Place a plate on top of the sandwich and weigh it down with several heavy objects (such as books) for 10 to 15 minutes. Slice into four squares and enjoy immediately or wrap tightly in plastic wrap to enjoy later.

SPECIAL INGREDIENT

Chinese eggplant are the small, long, and skinny variety. Their skins are thinner and they have little to no seeds, which make them my choice over globe eggplant.

COOKING SCHOOL

This isn't exactly rocket science, but it's worth noting that the sandwich is layered in the order listed for a reason. The veggies are juicy, and, when pressed, they'll release their juices. Bookending the vegetables—with the prosciutto on one side and the spinach on the other—creates a barrier so the bread doesn't get soggy.

Artichoke Tapenade

Tapenade is a spread made by finely chopping olives, capers, and varying other ingredients into a chunky paste. Artichokes, Parmesan cheese, and Dijon mustard play starring roles in making this version really special. It's wonderful as an appetizer spread over crostini or crackers and topped with a sprinkle of feta and fresh parsley, but I really love it on sandwiches—whether simply a baguette with mayonnaise and rotisserie chicken or my Grilled Vegetable and Prosciutto Sandwiches (facing page).

MAKES ABOUT 1½ CUPS [ABOUT 350 G]

12 oz [340 g] jarred artichoke hearts

⅓ cup [10 g] grated Parmesan cheese

2 garlic cloves, roughly chopped

2 Tbsp extra-virgin olive oil

1 Tbsp capers

1 Tbsp fresh lemon juice (from about ½ lemon)

1 tsp whole-grain Dijon mustard

⅛ tsp red pepper flakes

Dash of cayenne pepper

In a food processor or blender, combine all the ingredients and process until chopped very finely. Refrigerate in an airtight glass container for up to 1 week.

SPECIAL INGREDIENT

Capers seem to be one of those ingredients that lurk in the back of every refrigerator after being used once for a recipe. Don't neglect yours; they're basically little salt bombs—yum! Try adding them to Mushroom Ragu (see page 162), Crispy Chicken Thighs with Shallots and Nectarines (page 174), or to the mustard butter you pour over your pan-seared asparagus (see page 219).

Open-Faced Flank Steak Sandwich with Blue Cheese Sauce

Grilled flank steak is our go-to dinner party food—it's quick, simple, inexpensive, and so delicious. We always buy more than necessary so we can make steak sandwiches for lunch the next day. George invented this sandwich using leftover blue cheese from a cheese board we'd served at a dinner party one night, and now, thanks to this sandwich, we look forward even more to leftovers than to flank steak straight off the grill.

SERVES 2 GENEROUSLY

FOR THE FLANK STEAK

¼ red onion, thinly sliced, or 2 Tbsp Pickled Red Onions (page 82) if they're sitting in your fridge!

1 Tbsp champagne vinegar

8 oz [230 g] beef flank steak

¾ tsp kosher salt

¼ tsp freshly ground black pepper

2 Tbsp olive oil

1 ciabatta loaf

2 cups [40 g] arugula

1 Tbsp fresh lemon juice (from about ½ lemon)

FOR THE BLUE CHEESE SAUCE

4 oz [115 g] blue cheese, crumbled

2 Tbsp extra-virgin olive oil

2 Tbsp mayonnaise

2 Tbsp champagne vinegar

2 Tbsp water

1 Tbsp whole-grain Dijon mustard

To make the flank steak: In a small bowl, combine the red onion with enough water to cover and add the vinegar. Set aside.

Remove the steak from the refrigerator and let it come to room temperature for 30 minutes before cooking.

Heat a 12-in [30-cm] skillet (preferably cast iron) over medium-high heat. Season the flank steak with ½ tsp of the salt and the pepper. Rub it all over

with 1 Tbsp of the olive oil. Cook the steak for 9 to 10 minutes total, flipping once when the first side has a good charred crust, after 5 to 6 minutes. This is a chance to use your instant-read meat thermometer! For medium-rare steak, pull it off the heat when the thermometer registers 135°F [60°C]. Transfer the steak to a cutting board to rest while you prepare the rest of the sandwich.

continued

Slice the ciabatta in half horizontally, so you have an equal-size top and bottom. Drizzle the bottom half with the remaining 1 Tbsp olive oil and toast (however you normally toast your bread, but careful with the oil when using a conventional toaster) until lightly browned. Make sure it doesn't get too toasted, or it'll be hard to eat! Reserve the other ciabatta half for another use.

To make the blue cheese sauce: In a blender or mini food processor, combine the blue cheese, olive oil, mayonnaise, vinegar, water, and mustard. Blend on high speed until smooth. You will likely have to scrape down the sides of the blender bowl several times.

Cut the steak against the grain (see Cooking School) into very, very thin slices. Even if you don't get perfect slices, focus on getting those steak slices as thin as you can—it will make the sandwich so much easier to eat!

Place the toasted bread cut-side up on a cutting board and drizzle with 3 Tbsp of sauce. Drain the onion and place it in a large bowl. Add the arugula, lemon juice, and the remaining ¼ tsp of the salt. Toss to combine. Scatter the arugula mixture over the bread. Drizzle a bit more sauce over the top and arrange the steak slices over the arugula. Drizzle with a bit more sauce. Cut into two or four pieces and serve immediately.

LEFTOVERS ARE A GOOD THING

Use the remaining ciabatta to make croutons (use the Crunchy Croutons recipe (see page 104), but feel free to omit the chipotle. Or use both halves if you want a classic sandwich. Refrigerate leftover flank steak and blue cheese sauce separately in airtight containers for up to 3 days.

DO YOUR THING

I'm purposefully ambiguous in telling you how much blue cheese dressing to use on your sandwich. Everyone likes different levels of sauciness. If you have leftover sauce at the end, thin it with a bit more water and use as a salad dressing or crudités dip. Hate blue cheese? Use the Honey-Mustard Goat Cheese Spread (see page 133) instead.

COOKING SCHOOL

Cutting "against the grain" is really important to achieve a tender cut of steak. To do so, identify the direction of the lines of muscle fibers (the "grain") and cut perpendicular to them, rather than parallel with them. This makes the steak easier to chew, as the muscle fiber has already been broken up for you.

Patty Melts with Caramelized Onions and Smoked Gouda

A patty melt is basically a grilled cheese and a burger rolled into one. Prepare to be adored.

SERVES 2

FOR THE CARAMELIZED ONIONS

1 Tbsp unsalted butter, plus more for the pan

2 tsp olive oil

1 large yellow onion, thinly sliced

¼ cup [60 ml] red wine (any kind works)

FOR THE PATTY MELTS

2 Tbsp mayonnaise

1 Tbsp Dijon mustard

4 slices sourdough bread

8 oz [230 g] 90%/10% ground beef

Kosher salt

Freshly ground black pepper

1 Tbsp unsalted butter

1 Tbsp olive oil

4 slices smoked Gouda cheese

To make the caramelized onions: In a large skillet over high heat, melt the butter and olive oil. Add the onion and cook for 4 to 5 minutes, stirring frequently. Turn the heat to low and cook for 30 minutes more, stirring every 4 minutes or so.

Add the red wine and bring to a boil over high heat. Turn the heat to medium and cook for 4 to 5 minutes, stirring frequently, until all the wine has evaporated. Remove from the heat and set aside.

To make the patty melts: In a small bowl, stir together the mayonnaise and mustard and spread it on one side of each bread slice.

Form the beef into two patties and season generously with salt and pepper. In a large skillet over medium-high heat, melt the butter. Add the patties, several inches apart, and cook for 2 minutes per side.

They should still be slightly rare inside. Transfer to a plate and lower the heat to medium.

Wipe out the skillet with a clean paper towel.

Add the olive oil to the skillet and place two slices of bread into the skillet, Dijonnaise-side up. Top each with 1 slice of Gouda, a patty, 3 Tbsp of onions, another slice of Gouda, and, finally, a slice of bread, Dijonnaise-side down. Use a spatula to press down firmly on each sandwich. Cook for 1 to 2 minutes per side, until the bread is golden brown. Transfer the patty melts to two plates and cut in half to serve.

MAKE IT A MEAL

Patty melts are great for lunch or dinner. Serve them with kale tossed in Apple Cider Vinaigrette (page 91) for a lighter side, or Beet and Potato Hash (page 218) for something more substantial.

Party

DRINKS
AND BITES

Spending time with friends and family as a married couple is fun and enriching, but entertaining can seem intimidating. But with the right recipes, it's easy to pull off a fun, relaxed get-together at home. This chapter arms you with a collection of impressive cocktails, dips, and small bites to help you host a completely stress-free soirée, whether you're serving Pimiento Cheese (page 128) and beer at a game-day tailgate or mixing up Cherry Manhattans (facing page) for a pre-gala fête.

Cherry Manhattan

I've always viewed the ability to make a good Manhattan as a suave skill. Turns out, it's pretty much the easiest drink—ever—to make.

SERVES 2

½ cup [120 ml] bourbon

2 fl oz [60 ml] vermouth

4 tsp liquid from Bourbon-Soaked Cherries (recipe follows)

4 Bourbon Soaked Cherries (recipe follows)

Fill two short rocks glasses with ice. Divide the bourbon, vermouth, cherry liquid, and cherries between the glasses and stir to combine. Enjoy immediately.

LEFTOVERS ARE A GOOD THING

Spoon leftover Bourbon-Soaked Cherries over Pistachio Ice Cream (page 259) for the simplest, boozy dessert.

DO YOUR THING

For a traditional Manhattan, replace the soaked cherries and their juice with a dash of bitters.

BACK POCKET RECIPE

Bourbon-Soaked Cherries

Buy the best dried cherries you can find, soak them in bourbon and warm spices overnight, and you've got the most delicious cocktail garnish imaginable.

MAKES ½ CUP [70 G] CHERRIES

½ cup [70 g] dried Bing or Montmorency cherries

½ cup [120 ml] bourbon

1 vanilla bean

One 4-in [2.5-cm] cinnamon stick

1 star anise pod

In a covered container, combine the cherries, bourbon, vanilla bean, cinnamon stick, and star anise pod. Cover and shake to combine. Refrigerate for at least 12 hours before using.

Frozen Watermelon Margarita

George's work brought us to Manhattan for a summer—a brutally hot New York summer. It was the kind of summer where no amount of air conditioning can save you from humidity doom. The frozen watermelon margaritas across the street from our apartment at the Soho Grand were the only antidote. I share my take on the drink here—they'll be great for your next summer get-together.

SERVES 2

3 fl oz [90 ml] blanco tequila (or whatever tequila you have)

1 fl oz [30 ml] triple sec

3 Tbsp fresh lime juice (from about 2 limes)

1 lb [455 g] watermelon chunks, plus slices for garnishing

2 to 3 cups [400 to 600 g] ice

Pinch of kosher salt

Agave nectar for sweetening (optional)

In a blender, combine the tequila, triple sec, lime juice, watermelon, ice, and salt. Blend on high speed for 30 seconds, or until smooth. Add more ice if you want a thicker frozen consistency. Add 1 tsp of agave nectar at a time (if you want it sweeter). Serve in chilled cups with a slice of fresh watermelon.

DO YOUR THING

Swap tequila for rum and bit of fresh mint for a frozen watermelon mojito.

MAKE IT A MEAL

Kick off your fiesta with a pitcher of watermelon margaritas and set out a Chipotle Carnitas Tacos (page 206) buffet. Olé!

Jam Cocktails

Jam cocktails are the easiest way to achieve fresh fruit flavor with practically zero work. Try subbing in whatever jam you have sitting in your refrigerator—it's hard to go wrong. I especially love using fresh, locally made jams that I collect at the farmers' market. Scale this recipe up for however many guests you need to serve; just stir vigorously in a pitcher instead of shaking in a cocktail shaker.

Fig and Bourbon Cocktail

Despite living in frighteningly small spaces for the first many years of our marriage, George and I have always loved entertaining together. It's really fun to go beyond the typical beer or wine offering and be able to demonstrate your mixology skills to guests, and jam cocktails make playing bartender a breeze. This fig and bourbon cocktail is mildly sweet and so refreshing.

SERVES 2

2 Tbsp fig jam

2 Tbsp fresh lemon juice (from about 1 lemon)

3 fl oz [90 ml] bourbon

¼ tsp vanilla extract

1 tsp honey (optional)

In a cocktail shaker, combine the jam, lemon juice, bourbon, and vanilla with enough ice to fill the shaker. Cover and shake vigorously for 20 seconds. Taste. If it needs to be sweeter, add the honey (if you like). Re-cover and shake to combine. Alternatively, you can combine everything in a pitcher and stir to combine. Strain into two rocks glasses full of ice. Serve immediately.

SEASONALITY

The fun thing about using jam or preserves in cocktails is that you can serve a fig and bourbon cocktail in the middle of winter, or an orange and vodka cocktail in the middle of the summer! No fresh fruit needed to create a super-refreshing cocktail.

DO YOUR THING

Jam sweetness varies per brand, and even per batch, if you're buying an artisan jam that relies on fresh local fruit. Taste and add more honey, if needed.

Blackberry Bramble Fizz

Try setting out a DIY jam cocktail bar for your next event. This way, guests can make their own cocktails, leaving you free to mingle. Make a pretty display with an assortment of local jams, freshly squeezed lime and lemon juices, soda water, an ice bucket, and all the favorite liquors, including gin, bourbon, and vodka. If your guests need suggestions, this Blackberry Bramble Fizz is a great place to start.

SERVES 2

2 Tbsp blackberry jam

2 Tbsp fresh lime juice (from about 1 lime)

3 fl oz [90 ml] gin

1 tsp honey (optional)

½ cup [120 ml] soda water

In a cocktail shaker, combine the jam, lime juice, and gin with enough ice to fill the shaker. Cover and shake vigorously for 20 seconds. Taste. If it needs to be sweeter, add the honey (if you like). Re-cover and shake to combine. Alternatively, you can combine everything in a pitcher and stir to combine. Strain into two highball glasses full of ice. Stir in the soda water. Serve immediately.

SPECIAL INGREDIENT

Try mixing a scoop of blackberry jam into your morning yogurt and granola, serve it alongside cheese and crackers, or swirl it into the Lime Pie (page 255).

DO YOUR THING

Use Strawberry Rose Chia Jam (page 34) in place of the blackberry jam in this recipe. Sure, you'll have chia seeds floating around in your cocktail, but that makes the whole thing healthy, right?

Beet Tzatziki

This beet tzatziki is one of the most beautiful and simultaneously intriguing-looking dishes I make. This BRIGHT PINK dip is so simple, quite a conversation piece, and absolutely delicious as an appetizer with pita, or served alongside fried eggs, or as a sauce with grilled chicken . . . I could go on and on.

MAKES ABOUT 3 CUPS [ABOUT 475 G]

8 oz [230 g] beet (about 1 large beet), peeled and quartered

3 small garlic cloves

1 cup [240 g] plain Greek yogurt

1 Tbsp champagne vinegar

2 Tbsp finely chopped fresh dill

¼ tsp kosher salt

⅛ tsp freshly ground black pepper

Preheat the oven to 400°F [200°C].

Wrap the beet and garlic cloves in an aluminum foil packet. Place the packet on a baking sheet and roast for 45 minutes to 1 hour, or until a knife easily slides through the beet.

While the beet and garlic roast, in a small bowl, stir together the yogurt, vinegar, and dill.

Let the beet cool slightly. Grate it on a box grater and smash the roasted garlic into a paste with a fork. Stir the beet and garlic into the yogurt mixture. Season with the salt and pepper. Keep refrigerated in an airtight glass container for up to 4 days.

COOKING SCHOOL

Cutting beets into smaller pieces helps them roast faster. This goes for any vegetable, or cut of meat, for that matter.

BUY SMART

You can buy precooked beets in the refrigerator section in most major grocery stores. Totally acceptable. If you go this route, just grate in one clove of fresh garlic instead of roasting it.

Pimiento Cheese

Every good Southerner has a favorite pimiento cheese recipe. I had to lighten mine up a bit when we moved west, since Californians were terrified of my family's original recipe (which includes evaporated milk)! Pimiento cheese is delicious on crackers, but there's nothing better than a good ole pimiento cheese sandwich on white bread with the crusts cut off.

MAKES 3 CUPS [720 G]

4 oz [115 g] mild Cheddar cheese

8 oz [230 g] sharp Cheddar cheese

2 oz [55 g] jar diced pimientos, or ¼ cup [35 g] diced roasted red peppers

½ cup [120 g] mayonnaise, plus more as needed

2 Tbsp plain yogurt

½ tsp kosher salt

½ tsp freshly ground black pepper

½ tsp sugar

Dash of Worcestershire sauce

Use the largest hole on a box grater to grate the mild Cheddar cheese and the sharp Cheddar cheese into the bowl of a stand mixer or a large bowl you'll use with a handheld mixer. Add the pimientos, mayonnaise, yogurt, salt, pepper, sugar, and Worcestershire sauce. Mix for 1 to 2 minutes on low speed until fully incorporated. If you like your pimiento cheese "wetter," add more mayonnaise. This makes a large portion of pimiento cheese—halve the recipe if it's just the two of you. Keep refrigerated in an airtight container for up to 5 days. Let come to room temperature (30 minutes on the countertop) before serving.

DO YOUR THING

Try green olives or pickled jalapeño chiles instead of pimientos for a flavor twist.

MAKE IT A MEAL

In Chapel Hill, North Carolina, the restaurant at the historic Carolina Inn serves a BLT with a fried green tomato and a hefty portion of pimiento cheese. It's melty and gooey and absolutely delicious. A scoop of pimiento cheese on a burger is also a great decision.

Eggplant and Green Tomato Chutney

My mom is the queen of canning, or "putting up" as we call it in the South. Chutney is her forte, and she spends the summer and early autumn months sautéing and simmering up a storm. One summer, while George was on deployment, I came home to visit my parents, just as Mom's garden was really going wild—producing more than we could ever consume. After gorging ourselves on fried green tomatoes, we came up with this chutney recipe. It was an instant hit; everyone in our family now begs for a jar every time Mom comes to visit.

MAKES 2 CUPS [600 G]

One 2-lb [910-g] globe eggplant

1 Tbsp plus 2 tsp olive oil

2 cups [400 g] diced green tomatoes

2 shallots, minced

2 garlic cloves, minced

½ cup [120 ml] balsamic vinegar

¼ cup [85 g] honey

¼ cup [35 g] golden raisins

2 Tbsp fresh cilantro stems, finely chopped

2 Tbsp mustard seeds

1 tsp salt

1 tsp freshly ground black pepper

Preheat the oven to 400°F [200°C].

Halve the eggplant vertically and deeply score the flesh in a diamond pattern: Make about 8 deep parallel cuts, rotate 90 degrees, and make 8 more cuts perpendicular to the first set. Brush each half with 1 tsp of the olive oil. Place the eggplant halves cut-side down on a baking sheet and roast for 50 minutes. Let cool, scoop out the flesh, and chop it.

Meanwhile, in a large skillet over medium-high heat, heat the remaining 1 Tbsp olive oil. Add the green tomatoes, shallots, and garlic. Sauté for 7 to 10 minutes, until most of the moisture evaporates.

Stir in the eggplant, vinegar, honey, raisins, cilantro, mustard seeds, salt, and pepper. Turn the heat to medium-low and simmer for 10 minutes, uncovered.

Remove from the heat and let cool completely. Refrigerate in an airtight glass container for up to 1 month.

MAKE IT A MEAL

Serve this chutney alongside fish or chicken, over a wheel of warmed Brie, on a turkey sandwich, or with crackers.

SEASONALITY

Use tomatillos if you can't find green tomatoes.

Burrata with Garlic Confit

There is, perhaps, no cheese more universally loved than Burrata. It's been beloved fare at Italian restaurants for ages but has more recently become popular, and even expected, on menus everywhere. Lucky for us, it's finally becoming mainstream on grocery store shelves, and it's simple to make a gorgeous restaurant-quality appetizer spread using it at home. If you don't have time to make the Garlic Confit (facing page), just chop up some fresh tomatoes or even fresh pears to go alongside.

SERVES 4 TO 6 AS AN APPETIZER, 2 TO 4 AS A SIDE

1 large (8-oz [230-g]) ball Burrata cheese

4 thick slices country bread

1 Tbsp olive oil

½ cup [10 g] baby arugula

10 to 15 cloves Garlic Confit (facing page), warmed, plus 1 Tbsp Garlic Confit oil

1 tsp Maldon sea salt

Remove the Burrata cheese from the refrigerator at least 10 minutes before you're ready to serve.

Preheat a grill, or a grill pan, to medium heat.

Drizzle the bread slices on both sides with olive oil. Grill for 1 to 2 minutes per side with the lid open, until golden brown and with dark grill marks. Do not leave your bread unattended—it burns quickly! Transfer the bread to one side of a serving platter.

Mound the arugula on the other side of the platter and place the Burrata ball on top. Top with the warm garlic confit cloves and a good drizzle of its garlicky oil. Sprinkle the salt over the top and serve immediately.

LEFTOVERS ARE A GOOD THING

You'll have lots of leftover garlic. Try your hand at bread making with my Garlic Confit and Thyme Dutch Oven Bread (page 132).

MAKE IT A MEAL

Use 2 cups [40 g] of arugula, cut the bread into croutons, and add a chopped heirloom tomato for a cheese-heavy caprese-ish salad.

TOOL TIP

If you don't have a grill or a grill pan, just toast your bread as you normally would, being careful with the oil in a conventional toaster.

Garlic Confit

Warning: You may find yourself wanting to put garlic on everything . . . but I caution restraint on date night! Garlic confit is garlic that has been slowly cooked in hot oil. It's versatile, too—smashed and mixed into mayonnaise as a sandwich spread, served over fresh Burrata cheese (facing page), or even cooked into a fresh loaf of Garlic Confit and Thyme Dutch Oven Bread (page 132). You'll have no shortage of ways to use garlic confit, and it keeps in the refrigerator for up to 1 month.

MAKES ABOUT 1 CUP [150 G] GARLIC IN 1 CUP [240 ML] OLIVE OIL

1 cup [150 g] peeled garlic cloves

2 fresh rosemary sprigs

2 fresh thyme sprigs

1 cup [240 ml] olive oil

In a small pot over the lowest heat possible, cook the garlic, rosemary, thyme, and olive oil for 25 to 30 minutes. The garlic cloves should not brown at all; if they start to darken, remove the pot from the heat immediately.

Remove the herbs and transfer the oil and garlic to an airtight glass container. Refrigerate for up to 1 month. Before use, bring to room temperature, since the oil solidifies in the refrigerator.

Garlic Confit and Thyme Dutch Oven Bread

There's nothing quite as comforting as the smell of freshly baked bread. Garlic confit and fresh thyme leaves punctuate this crusty-on-the-outside, pillowy-on-the-inside quick yeast bread.

MAKES 1 LOAF

1½ cups [360 ml] warm water

1 tsp active dry yeast

1 tsp honey

2 cups [280 g] all-purpose flour, plus more for dusting

2 cups [280 g] bread flour

1 Tbsp fresh thyme leaves

2 tsp kosher salt

20 cloves Garlic Confit (page 131), halved, rinsed, and patted dry

3 Tbsp olive oil

Maldon sea salt

In a small bowl, stir together the water, yeast, and honey. Set aside for 3 to 5 minutes, until foamy.

In a stand mixer fitted with the hook attachment, or in a large bowl with a handheld mixer, combine the all-purpose flour, bread flour, thyme, and salt. Mix on low speed to combine. With the mixer running on medium speed, slowly pour in the yeast mixture. Mix for 8 minutes. After 1 minute, scrape down the sides and bottom of the bowl to make sure all the flour is incorporated. The dough will be smooth and no longer sticky when it's ready. With the mixer on low speed, add the garlic and mix for a couple of seconds just to incorporate. Remove the bowl from the stand mixer, pick up the dough with your clean hands, and spray the bowl with nonstick cooking spray, or coat with 1 Tbsp olive oil. Return the dough to the bowl, cover, and let rise in a warm place for 2 to 4 hours.

Turn the dough out onto a floured surface and knead for 2 minutes. Let the dough rest for 5 minutes, roll it into a tight ball, and transfer it to a lidded Dutch oven that has been oiled with 1 Tbsp olive oil. Cover the pot and let the dough rise for 30 to 60 minutes

Preheat the oven to 450°F [230°C].

Remove the Dutch oven lid, rub the top of the dough with 1 Tbsp olive oil, and sprinkle with salt. Cut a large X across the top. Put the lid on and bake for 30 minutes. After 30 minutes, remove the lid, lower the oven temperature to 375°F [190°C], and bake for 15 minutes more, or until the bread is golden brown and has an internal temperature of 200°F [95°C].

Let cool completely, then wrap in plastic wrap and store at room temperature for up to 4 days, or wrap in aluminum foil and freeze for up to 1 month.

DO YOUR THING

Omit the garlic confit if you want great plain bread. Or, try dried cherries and rosemary, or raisins and walnuts, or olives.

Sweet Potato Biscuits with Prosciutto, Honey-Mustard Goat Cheese, and Arugula

My grandmother raised five children and still managed to host beautiful dinner parties regularly for her friends and family. Her sweet potato biscuits are a timeless, sure-thing crowd pleaser. I dress them up a bit with a sweet-and-savory goat cheese sauce, prosciutto, and arugula. They're still my mom's go-to contribution to any potluck dinner. They may now become yours, too.

MAKES 10 (2-IN [5-CM]) BISCUITS

FOR THE SWEET POTATO BISCUITS

One 8-oz [230 g] sweet potato, peeled and cut into ½-in [12-mm] rounds

3 Tbsp unsalted butter, at room temperature, plus 1 Tbsp unsalted butter, melted

1¼ cups [175 g] all-purpose flour, plus more for dusting

2 Tbsp light brown sugar

1 Tbsp baking powder

½ tsp kosher salt

2 Tbsp milk, as needed

1 tsp Maldon sea salt

FOR THE HONEY-MUSTARD GOAT CHEESE SPREAD

4 oz [115 g] goat cheese, at room temperature

2 Tbsp Dijon mustard

1 Tbsp honey

4 oz [115 g] prosciutto slices

½ cup [10 g] baby arugula

Preheat the oven to 450°F [230°C] and position a rack in the upper third of the oven. Line a baking sheet with aluminum foil and set aside.

To make the sweet potato biscuits: Place the sweet potato slices in a small pot or saucepan and cover with 1 in [2.5 cm] of water. Bring to a boil over high heat. Turn the heat to low and simmer for 20 to 25 minutes, or until very soft. Drain and transfer the

sweet potato slices to a large bowl. Add the 3 Tbsp room-temperature butter and mash together.

In a separate large bowl, whisk the flour, brown sugar, baking powder, and kosher salt. Add the flour mixture to the sweet potato mixture and use your clean hands to combine. If the dough holds together when pinched, it's ready. If not, stir in 1 tsp of milk at a time until the dough holds together when pinched.

continued

The amount of milk needed will depend on how moist your potatoes are.

Sprinkle a clean work surface with flour. Use clean hands to gather the dough into a ball and transfer it to the floured surface. Knead the dough into a smooth ball and use your hands to lightly pat the dough into a 1-in- [2.5-cm-] thick round. Use a 2-in [5-cm] biscuit cutter to cut out 10 biscuits from the dough, re-rolling the scraps a maximum of two times.

Place the biscuits 2 in [5 cm] apart on the prepared baking sheet. Use a pastry brush to coat the biscuit tops with the 1 Tbsp melted butter and sprinkle with the sea salt. Bake for 10 to 12 minutes, or until the biscuit tops are golden brown. They will not rise significantly like other biscuits.

While the biscuits bake, make the honey-mustard goat cheese spread: In a small bowl, stir together the goat cheese, Dijon mustard, and honey. The spread will look lumpy at first; keep stirring until smooth.

Let the biscuits cool slightly, halve them, and spread the goat cheese mixture over the biscuit bottoms. Divide the prosciutto and arugula evenly among the biscuits. Put the tops on the biscuits and serve.

DO YOUR THING

Use a 4-in [10-cm] biscuit cutter to make breakfast biscuits. Pile them high with scrambled eggs, Cheddar cheese, and bacon.

COOKING SCHOOL

Biscuit bottoms burning? Place another baking sheet underneath the one the biscuits are on; your oven heat is just baking too strongly from the bottom, but this will fix it.

MAKE AHEAD

Make the dough as much as 48 hours before baking the biscuits. Allow the dough to come up to room temperature and cut into biscuits before baking, otherwise add a couple of minutes to the cook time.

Pan con Tomate, a.k.a. Tomato Bread

The Spaniards have been doing "toast" since before toast was $10 and came with a side of hipster cafe snark. When I studied in Seville, Spain, my junior year of college, I ate this every morning for breakfast at the cafe at my university, usually while Skyping George. They actually just cut the tomato in half and rub it on the bread, but my grating method provides a much heftier portion of tomato, which I love. Almost ten years later, and we're still weaving this recipe into our married-life entertaining.

SERVES 4 TO 6

4 thick slices sourdough bread

1 Tbsp olive oil

2 garlic cloves

1 perfectly ripe large tomato, grated on the large holes of a box grater

1 Tbsp extra-virgin olive oil

Maldon sea salt

Red pepper flakes for seasoning

Preheat the oven to broil.

Drizzle the bread slices on both sides with olive oil and toast them under the broiler for 2 to 3 minutes per side, or until golden brown. Watch closely, because the bread can burn quickly!

Rub the raw garlic cloves over both sides of the toasted bread. Spoon the tomato evenly over the toast slices, drizzle with the olive oil, and season with salt and red pepper flakes.

DO YOUR THING

Serve this as-is for a substantial appetizer, snack, or breakfast, or cut each piece of toast into four pieces for a rustic canapé.

MAKE AHEAD

Making this dish ahead of time is a no-go since the bread will get soggy. For easy entertaining, simply grate the tomato into the center of a dish, season it with salt and pepper, and surround it with olive oil and balsamic vinegar. Serve with lots of crusty bread and let your guests build their own pan con tomate–inspired crostini.

Pineapple and Shrimp Ceviche

Ceviche is the ultimate summertime food—absolutely zero heat is required, because the acid in the citrus juice takes care of the "cooking." A bit of chopping and squeezing is all you need to create this tropics-inspired ceviche. Onion and radishes add crunch, avocado adds a bit of fatty creaminess to cut through all of the acidic citrus, and serrano spices it up.

SERVES 2 AS A MEAL, 4 TO 6 AS AN APPETIZER

1 lb [455 g] raw shrimp, any size, shelled and deveined, cut into ¼-in [6-mm] pieces

Juice of 3 limes

Juice of 2 oranges

1 cup [155 g] diced fresh pineapple

½ small white onion, finely diced (about ¼ cup [35 g])

1 serrano chile, seeded and finely diced

4 radishes, quartered and thinly sliced

1 small avocado, diced

½ cup [20 g] roughly chopped fresh cilantro

Tortilla chips for serving

Small butter lettuce leaves for serving

In a large bowl, combine the shrimp, lime juice, and orange juice. Cover tightly and refrigerate to marinate for at least 1 hour, or overnight.

Drain the shrimp and place in a clean large bowl. Add the pineapple, onion, serrano chile, radishes, avocado, and cilantro. Toss to combine. Transfer to a serving bowl and serve with tortilla chips and/or butter lettuce leaves for scooping.

DO YOUR THING

Substitute fresh scallops or any semi-firm white-fleshed fish for the shrimp. Mango is wonderful in place of the pineapple.

MAKE IT A MEAL

This ceviche recipe makes a wonderful light meal for two. Serve with lots of butter lettuce leaves or warm soft corn tortillas to make wraps.

Oysters with Raspberry Mignonette

Scotland is one of George and my favorite places on earth—we love the scenery, the moody weather, and the abundance of fresh, simple food. One of my favorite meals was eating oysters in the pouring rain, at a little shack with just a handwritten sign that said OYSTERS, perched on a hill overlooking the lake on Isle of Skye. They had the most delicious home-made mignonettes. This recipe is inspired by one we tried that day.

SERVES 2

½ cup [60 g] fresh raspberries

½ cup [120 ml] champagne vinegar

1 Tbsp diced shallot

1 Tbsp extra-virgin olive oil

Pinch of kosher salt

Pinch of freshly ground black pepper

12 fresh oysters

In a high-powered blender, combine the raspberries and vinegar. Blend on high speed for 30 seconds. Pour the raspberry mixture into a large bowl. Stir in the shallot, olive oil, salt, and pepper. Cover and refrigerate for at least 1 hour, or up to 2 days.

Open the oysters, and serve immediately on the half shell, each dressed with ½ tsp raspberry mignonette.

DO YOUR THING

Serve the oysters on a flat, rimmed serving platter covered in ice for a gorgeous and food-safe presentation. On the side, have bowls of this mignonette, lemon wedges, cocktail sauce, and saltines.

COOKING SCHOOL

To open an oyster, lay it flat on a clean kitchen towel. Using a separate kitchen towel, press down firmly on the oyster, leaving the "hinge" side of the oyster exposed. Wedge the pointy tip of your oyster knife into the hinge and twist to pry the oyster open. Some oysters are really briny and the shells will break apart when you try to open them—don't give up, just keep prying until it opens!

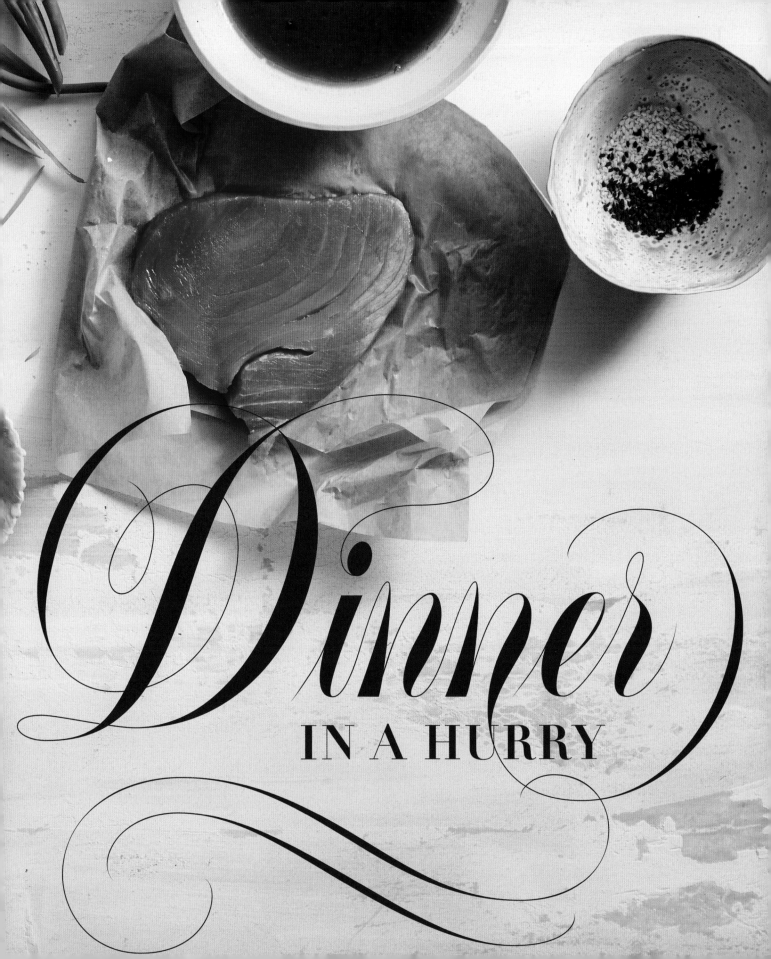

Dinner
IN A HURRY

Listen, I get it. Some nights, after a particularly long day, standing in the kitchen cooking for an hour sounds like the most impossible feat imaginable . . . even when you're sharing the duty. We've all been there. These dinner-in-a-hurry recipes are here for you on those nights when you just need to eat dinner as quickly as possible so you can cuddle up on the couch watching 30 *Rock* reruns before you pass out by 9 p.m. (I just described our average Wednesday night.)

In this chapter, there are recipes that take advantage of store-bought rotisserie chicken (Rotisserie Chicken Two Ways, page 152), recipes that prove tomato sauce doesn't have to simmer all day to be absolutely delicious (Shells with Creamy Tomato Sauce, page 144), and poke bowls (Sesame Soy Tuna Poke Bowls, page 149) that can be ready in 30 minutes and won't cost you $20 for a tiny scoop of fish!

Dal with Garlicky Yogurt

My dear friend Sarah met a Tibetan refugee at a hunger strike in India, fell in love, and eventually found a way to bring him to California and marry him (in one of the most beautiful weddings I've ever attended). Tashi is a wonderful cook and can whip up some version of dal (an Indian spiced lentil stew) even when there's seemingly nothing to eat in the house.

SERVES 2

2 Tbsp grapeseed oil

½ red onion, finely chopped

4 garlic cloves, minced, plus 1 garlic clove, grated

2 tsp minced peeled fresh ginger

½ tsp ground cumin

½ cup [100 g] red lentils

1 Roma tomato or other medium tomato, diced

1½ cups [360 ml] chicken broth or water

4 oz [115 g] ground beef

⅓ cup [80 g] plain yogurt or Greek yogurt

Kosher salt

Freshly ground black pepper

¼ cup [10 g] chopped fresh cilantro

In a large saucepan over medium heat, warm 1 Tbsp of the grapeseed oil. Add the onion, minced garlic, ginger, and cumin. Cook for 5 to 7 minutes, stirring frequently, until the onion is translucent.

Stir in the lentils, tomato, and chicken broth. Raise the heat to high to bring to a boil. Turn the heat to low, cover the pan, and cook for 15 to 20 minutes, until the lentils absorb most of the liquid and are completely soft.

Meanwhile, in a large nonstick skillet over medium-high heat, warm the remaining 1 Tbsp grapeseed oil. Add the beef and cook for 6 to 8 minutes, until cooked through, using a wooden spoon to chop it up into small pieces. When it's browned and cooked through, drain off any fat in the pan and set aside.

In a small bowl, stir together the grated garlic and yogurt. Season with a pinch of salt.

When the lentils are cooked, mix in the ground beef and season with salt and pepper. Stir in the cilantro and divide the dal between two bowls. Top each with a scoop of garlicky yogurt.

BUY SMART

You can buy exactly 4 oz [115 g] ground beef from the meat counter; pre-packaged containers are usually about 1 lb [455 g].

MAKE IT A MEAL

To make this meal more substantial, serve it over rice.

Shells with Creamy Tomato Sauce

Only four ingredients in this creamy tomato sauce are ones you might not regularly keep on hand, and it requires only about five minutes of active cooking time. The olive oil and pasta water emulsifies with the tomatoes, making the sauce smooth and luscious. I love using pasta shells because they pick up so much sauce in their nooks and crannies, but use whatever pasta you have on hand.

SERVES 2

¼ cup [60 ml] extra-virgin olive oil

1 pt (12 oz [340 g]) cherry tomatoes

¼ tsp kosher salt

8 oz [230 g] medium or small pasta shells

¼ cup [8 g] grated Parmesan cheese, plus more for garnishing

Pinch of red pepper flakes

½ cup [20 g] chiffonade fresh basil leaves (see Cooking School, page 40)

In a medium skillet over low heat, combine the olive oil, tomatoes, and salt. Simmer for 25 minutes, or until all tomatoes burst and begin to break down.

In a large pot over high heat, boil several quarts of heavily salted water. Time the cooking of your pasta so it finishes cooking around the time your pasta sauce is done. Cook the pasta until al dente; it should still have some chew when you test a piece. Drain, reserving ¼ cup [60 ml] of the pasta water.

Transfer the tomatoes and the reserved pasta water to a blender and blend on high speed for 15 seconds, or until smooth. Combine the pasta and tomato sauce in the cooking pot and place it over low heat. Gently stir in the Parmesan cheese until melted. Divide the pasta between two bowls and sprinkle with red pepper flakes and the basil.

DO YOUR THING

Blend ¼ cup [35 g] of roasted red peppers with the tomatoes for a more robust sauce. Add some Burrata cheese for a heartier meal.

COOKING SCHOOL

Adding the starchy leftover water from cooking pasta to your pasta sauce helps it thicken and stick to your pasta. If you have an immersion blender, blend the sauce right in the pot for easier cleanup.

Honey & Garlic Salmon

Daunted by the idea of cooking fish at home? This one-pan recipe is here to change your mind. After searing the salmon in a hot skillet, you make a simple honey-butter pan sauce, which reduces into a perfectly sticky sweet glaze as you continue to cook the salmon, basting it with the sauce as you go. This salmon has a lovely crispy sear on the outside, and is perfectly cooked on the inside.

SERVES 2

1 Tbsp olive oil

Two 4 to 6 oz [115 to 170 g] salmon fillets

½ tsp kosher salt

¼ tsp freshly ground black pepper

3 Tbsp unsalted butter

3 garlic cloves, grated

3 Tbsp honey

Juice of ½ lemon

Score the salmon skin by using a very sharp knife to make four 1-in [2.5-cm] lengthwise incisions. Do not cut past the skin. Season the fillets with salt and pepper. Allow them to come to room temperature by sitting unrefrigerated for at least 15 minutes.

Warm the olive oil in a 10-in [25-cm] nonstick skillet over medium-high heat. Place the salmon skin-side down in the hot skillet. Cook until the skin is crispy and golden brown, about 2 minutes.

Reduce the heat to low and flip the salmon over. Add the butter, garlic, and honey to the skillet, and stir with a spoon or spatula to combine. After 1 minute, flip the salmon back over to cook skin-side down. Baste with the honey butter.

Baste with the honey butter every 30 seconds or so. Cook until the salmon flakes easily when prodded with a fork, 6 to 7 minutes. Squeeze the lemon juice over the top and serve immediately.

COOKING SCHOOL

Cooking salmon with the skin on helps prevent over-cooking! The fatty skin protects the delicate, lean fish. Allowing fish, and other meats, to come to room temperature before cooking allows for a more even, perfect cook.

MAKE IT A MEAL

Serve this salmon with brown rice (see Quick Cooking Reference Guide, page 263) and Charred Broccoli (page 232) minus the Sriracha Almond Butter Sauce.

DO YOUR THING

The one-skillet cooking technique above provides a crispy sear, but maybe you prefer a completely tender, flaky fish? If so, cooking it low and slow is the way to go. To do so, preheat your oven to 250°F. Place the fattest salmon fillets you can find skin side down on a rimmed baking sheet and season them with salt and pepper. Melt the butter, and whisk it with the garlic and honey. Pour it over the fillets. Bake until the salmon is just opaque in the center, 15 to 20 minutes. This method renders the salmon fat slowly, and will result in a fillet that still looks raw, but is in fact cooked through!

Sesame Soy Tuna Poke Bowls

George and I honeymooned in Kauai and Maui, so poke has a very special place in our hearts. Poke is essentially raw fish diced and tossed with different sauces, traditionally soy sauce-based. After a morning of hiking or surfing, we found our way to a local fish counter almost every day for fresh Hawaiian poke.

SERVES 2

3 Tbsp soy sauce

1 Tbsp sesame oil

1 Tbsp rice vinegar

2 tsp Sriracha

1 Tbsp toasted sesame seeds

One 1-in [2.5-cm] piece peeled fresh ginger, grated

1 garlic clove, grated

1 lb [455 g] fresh ahi tuna fillet, cut into ½-in [12-mm] cubes

4 scallions, white and green parts, thinly sliced

SUGGESTED TOPPINGS

1 to 2 cups [120 to 240 g] cooked white rice (see Quick Cooking Reference Guide, page 263)

1 cup [60 g] shredded napa cabbage

1 avocado, thinly sliced

¼ cup [40 g] cooked and shelled edamame

¼ cup [10 g] shredded carrot

¼ cup [60 g] cubed cucumber

3 Tbsp store-bought pickled ginger

In a large bowl, whisk the soy sauce, sesame oil, vinegar, Sriracha, sesame seeds, ginger, and garlic. Toss in the cubed tuna, cover, and refrigerate to marinate while you cook the rice and prepare the toppings of your choice.

To prepare the bowls, divide the rice, tuna, and desired toppings (napa cabbage, avocado, edamame, carrot, cucumber, and pickled ginger) between two bowls. Enjoy immediately!

LEFTOVERS ARE A GOOD THING

Best to enjoy your poke right away, but it will keep, stored in an airtight glass container in the refrigerator, for up to 2 days.

DO YOUR THING

Make a spicy mayo poke instead of, or along with your sesame soy poke. Stir together 2 Tbsp mayonnaise, 1 Tbsp Sriracha, and 1 Tbsp sesame oil and toss with the cubed tuna.

BUY SMART

If you ask nicely, most fishmongers will cut your tuna into cubes for you. Buy shredded cabbage, shredded carrots, pre-cut cucumber, and cooked rice from the salad and hot bar if you're really trying to do as little work as possible.

Red Curry Mussels

My friend Grace hosts the most fabulous casual-feeling yet gourmet-tasting dinner parties. She's the type of host who doesn't put down her wineglass or leave the conversation once as she flits gracefully around the kitchen. These mussels are one of Grace's go-tos for an easy night in, and they have become beloved by all those lucky enough to be her dinner guests. The mussel broth is intensely flavorful, so be sure to serve it with lots of bread to soak up every last drop.

SERVES 2 AS A MEAL, 4 AS AN APPETIZER

One 13-oz [390-ml] can coconut milk

⅓ cup [80 ml] dry white wine

2 to 4 Tbsp [30 to 60 g] red curry paste

1 Tbsp fish sauce

2 tsp sugar

3 garlic cloves, grated

One 1-in [2.5-cm] piece peeled fresh ginger, grated

½ jalapeño chile, seeded and minced

2 lb [910 g] fresh mussels, scrubbed and debearded

¼ cup [10 g] chopped fresh cilantro

1 baguette, cut into ½-in [12-mm] slices

In a large saucepan or pot with a lid over high heat, stir together the coconut milk, white wine, red curry paste (the more, the spicier), fish sauce, sugar, garlic, ginger, and jalapeño. Bring to a boil; turn the heat to low, and simmer, uncovered, for 15 minutes.

Stir the mussels into the broth. Cover the pot and continue cooking for 8 to 12 minutes, until all mussels open. While the mussels cook, carefully shake the pan a few times to mix the mussels up and ensure they're not sticking to the bottom.

Pour the mussels and broth into a large shallow bowl, or serve them straight from the pot. Discard any mussels that didn't open, because this means they've gone bad. Sprinkle with the fresh cilantro and serve immediately with the baguette for sopping up all the coconut curry broth.

DO YOUR THING

Double the broth, and add 1 lb [455 g] of clams and 1 lb [455 g] of shrimp for a Thai seafood boil!

BUY SMART

Look carefully at the mussels before you buy them. If more than two are open or cracked, ask for a new bag.

Coconut Milk Shrimp

I come back to this recipe over and over because it's the perfect combination of spicy, creamy, and a little sweet and, most important, because I *always* have these ingredients on hand. Even if I have no fresh produce, I almost always have an onion lurking around, canned tomatoes (rather than fresh, as the recipe calls for), and frozen shrimp. I'll toss in snap peas or another fresh veggie if I have one, but the shrimp are so tasty all on their own. Once you learn to cook with coconut milk you'll find yourself constantly coming up with new ways to use it. (Bonus: This recipe is easy enough for the noncook in the family to tackle, too!)

SERVES 2

2 tsp grapeseed oil

½ small yellow onion, chopped

2 garlic cloves, minced

¾ cup [180 ml] coconut milk

¼ cup [60 ml] water

2 tsp fish sauce, or ½ tsp kosher salt

1 to 3 tsp sambal oelek (depending on how spicy you like it)

½ cup [90 g] seeded and diced Roma tomato (about 1 large tomato)

8 oz [230 g] shelled and deveined medium shrimp (12 to 15 shrimp)

1 cup [65 g] sugar snap peas

Steamed rice for serving

¼ cup [10 g] chopped fresh cilantro leaves

Lime wedges for serving

In a medium nonstick skillet over medium heat, warm the grapeseed oil. Add the onion and garlic and cook for 2 to 3 minutes, stirring frequently, until the onion is translucent.

Stir in the coconut milk, water, fish sauce, sambal oelek, and tomato. Bring to a boil over high heat. Cook for 4 to 5 minutes, stirring occasionally, until slightly reduced and thickened. Turn the heat to medium-low, add the shrimp and peas, and cook for 3 to 4 minutes, until the shrimp are cooked through and the peas are crisp-tender. Remove from the heat.

Divide between two bowls and serve with steamed rice and garnish with the fresh cilantro and a lime wedge or two.

DO YOUR THING

Use curry paste in place of sambal oelek for a quick shrimp curry.

SPECIAL INGREDIENT

Yes, coconut milk is high in calories. But it's also high in important vitamins and minerals, plus the rest of the ingredients in this dish are low enough in calories that it balances out. Use leftover coconut milk to make a Green Piña Colada Smoothie tomorrow morning (page 29).

Rotisserie Chicken

When I'm really busy, rotisserie chickens are always on my grocery list. Mealtime is a snap when half the dish is already (perfectly) cooked! Here I share two ways to dress up a rotisserie chicken in no time at all.

Chicken Labneh Flatbreads

Flatbread sandwiches and "pizzas" are the perfect canvas for leftovers to be reimagined. A little extra sauce from one recipe + some extra protein from another + a smattering of whatever cheese is left in the back of the fridge = dinner in under 10 minutes.

SERVES 2

¼ cup [60 g] labneh or Greek yogurt	2 round flatbreads or pocketless pitas
1 garlic clove, grated	½ store-bought, cooked rotisserie chicken
1 Tbsp fresh lemon juice (from about ½ lemon)	¼ cup [5 g] arugula
2 tsp olive oil	4 Tbsp [40 g] Pickled Red Onions (page 82)

Preheat the oven to 350°F [180°C].

In a small bowl, stir together the labneh, garlic, lemon juice, and olive oil. Warm the flatbreads in the oven for 3 to 5 minutes, or until pliable and warm.

Spread 2 Tbsp of the labneh mixture over each flatbread. Shred the chicken and place about ¼ cup [115 g] down the center of each flatbread. Divide the arugula between the 2 flatbreads and scatter 2 Tbsp of pickled red onions over the top of each. Enjoy immediately.

BUY SMART

Buy arugula from a bulk bin to get the perfect amount. Or, if you have to buy a box or bag, make a salad with chopped dates and Apple Cider Vinaigrette (page 91) as a side dish.

SPECIAL INGREDIENT

Labneh is made from straining the liquid out of full-fat yogurt. If you have the time, it's worth it to make your own labneh: Set a strainer lined with cheesecloth over a bowl, scoop the yogurt into it, and stir in a pinch of salt. Refrigerate overnight to drain. What remains in the strainer is the labneh. Voilà!

Cheesy Chicken Nachos

Some nights, having dinner on the table in less than 30 minutes and only one dish to wash can make these Cheesy Chicken Nachos—preferably eaten with your fingers, straight off the baking sheet—even more romantic than a four-course candlelit meal.

SERVES 2 AS A MEAL, 4 TO 6 AS AN APPETIZER

FOR THE NACHOS

½ small store-bought, cooked rotisserie chicken

One 9-oz [255-g] bag tortilla chips

½ small white onion, finely chopped (add the other half to the pico de gallo, if desired)

One 15-oz [430-g] can black beans

½ jalapeño, seeded and diced (add the other half to the pico de gallo, if desired)

8 oz [230 g] sharp Cheddar cheese, grated

FOR THE LIME CREMA

½ cup [120 g] sour cream

Juice of 1 lime

4 oz [115 g] feta cheese, crumbled

2 cups store-bought pico de gallo salsa

1 avocado, chopped

½ bunch fresh cilantro (leaves only), chopped

Preheat the oven to 350°F [180°C]. Coat a large rimmed baking sheet with nonstick cooking spray.

To make the nachos: Use your hands to pull the chicken off the bones and shred it into small pieces.

Arrange half the chips evenly over the prepared sheet. Top with half of the chicken, onion, black beans, jalapeño, and Cheddar cheese. Repeat with the remaining ingredients for a total of three layers. Bake for 10 to 15 minutes, until the cheese is melted and gooey.

While the nachos bake, make the lime crema: In a small bowl, stir together the sour cream and lime juice.

Remove the nachos from the oven and sprinkle with the feta, 1 cup of the pico de gallo, avocado, and cilantro. Serve straight on the baking sheet with the lime crema and remaining pico de gallo on the side.

LEFTOVERS ARE A GOOD THING

Pull the remaining half of the chicken and make Gochujang Chicken Salad (page 106), or mix it with a bit of mayo, sliced grapes, and diced celery for a classic chicken salad.

BUY SMART

Make a fruity pico de gallo by mixing diced fresh fruit into store-bought pico de gallo.

Spicy Eggplant and Pork Stir-Fry

Put down the phone—no need to order in Chinese food tonight! The biggest win of this recipe is the stir-fry sauce—use it with any combination of veggies and meat for a healthy, flavor-packed quick lunch or dinner. If you aren't familiar with cooking eggplant, this is a great recipe to start with, because it demonstrates how it absorbs flavors and how tender it can be when cooked over high heat.

SERVES 4

⅓ [80 ml] cup chicken broth

2 Tbsp rice vinegar

2 Tbsp soy sauce

2 Tbsp sambal oelek

1 Tbsp sesame oil

1 lb [455 g] ground pork

2 Tbsp grapeseed oil

1 lb [455 g] Chinese eggplant, cut into 2-by-½-in [5-cm-by-12-mm] matchsticks

1 large shallot, diced

2 large garlic cloves, thinly sliced

2 cups [40 g] fresh baby spinach

¼ cup [10 g] chopped fresh cilantro

In a small bowl, whisk the chicken broth, rice vinegar, soy sauce, and sambal oelek.

In a 12-in [30-cm] nonstick skillet over medium-high heat, add the sesame soil and cook the pork for 6 to 7 minutes, stirring with a wooden spoon to break up clumps, until cooked through. Add 2 Tbsp of the broth mixture and continue stirring until the liquid evaporates. Transfer the pork to a bowl and wipe out the skillet.

Return the skillet to medium-high heat and add 1 Tbsp of the grapeseed oil. When hot, add the eggplant and stir quickly to coat it in the oil before it sticks to the pan. Spread the eggplant in an even layer and cook for 1 minute. Stir it to flip it and cook for 1 minute more.

Add the shallot, garlic, and a splash of water and continue to cook for about 8 minutes, stirring, until the eggplant is brown and tender. Add a splash of water if the vegetables start to stick.

Add the remaining broth mixture and the pork to the skillet. Stir until most of the liquid is absorbed, about 2 minutes. Remove from the heat and stir in the spinach until wilted. Transfer to four plates and sprinkle with cilantro.

LEFTOVERS ARE A GOOD THING

I like to toss any leftovers over fresh spinach in a microwave-safe container for a delicious desk lunch tomorrow. I microwave the entire thing and the fresh spinach wilts and gives the leftovers a new life. Leftovers will keep for up to 3 days in the refrigerator.

Date Night IN

Any night can become date night with the right attitude. Even if you're sitting on the floor, eating off paper plates, sipping wine out of mismatched glasses, simply calling it "a date" can change the course of the entire evening. When your loved one gets the promotion, makes the deal, or simply deserves to be celebrated for being, pull out your best china, light a couple of candles, and cook a thick, buttery Cast Iron T-Bone with Red Wine Sauce (page 179). When you both crave a little indulgence, get in the kitchen together and make a pair of Sausage and Honey Pizzas (page 168). No matter the occasion, a special meal for two is always the best way to celebrate, and these recipes allow you to do so in the comfort of your home.

Creamy Corn Pasta

During the summer in North Carolina, you can buy corn for pennies at roadside stands. I look forward to summers for this pasta alone.

SERVES 2

8 oz [230 g] rotini or farfalle pasta

2 Tbsp unsalted butter

1 large shallot, diced

2 garlic cloves, thinly sliced

¼ cup [60 ml] water

3 large ears corn, husked, kernels removed (about 2¼ cups [315 g] kernels)

2 Tbsp fresh lemon juice (from about 1 lemon)

½ tsp kosher salt

⅓ cup [10 g] grated Parmesan cheese

¼ tsp red pepper flakes, plus more as needed

¼ cup [10 g] chiffonade fresh basil leaves (see Cooking School, page 40), plus more for garnishing

2 lemon wedges

In a large pot, bring salted water to a boil and cook the pasta until al dente, about 10 minutes. Reserve ½ cup [120 ml] of the cooking water and drain the pasta.

In a large sauté pan or skillet over medium-low heat, melt 1 Tbsp of the butter. Add the shallot and garlic and cook, stirring frequently, for 3 to 5 minutes, until the shallot is translucent. Add the water and all but ⅓ cup [45 g] corn and simmer for about 3 minutes, until tender. Transfer to a blender and add the lemon juice and ¼ tsp of the salt. Blend on high speed until smooth. Add a little of the reserved pasta water, if needed, to make it pourable and smooth.

Return the pan to medium-high heat and add the remaining 1 Tbsp butter. Add the reserved ⅓ cup [45 g] corn and cook for 1 to 2 minutes, until tender. Pour in the corn purée and stir together for about 30 seconds to combine.

Turn the heat to medium-low and toss in the cooked pasta. Toss to combine, adding additional splashes of the pasta water if the sauce seems too thick. Stir in the Parmesan, red pepper flakes, basil, and the remaining ¼ tsp salt. Season with additional salt and red pepper flakes, if desired.

Transfer the pasta to two bowls. Garnish with the basil and serve with a lemon wedge.

DO YOUR THING

Char the corn on the grill before removing the kernels to add a smoky depth to the pasta. Adjust your cook times accordingly—it won't need as much time on the stove, since it'll already be cooked.

MAKE IT A MEAL

The pasta is rich, so serve it with simple grilled shrimp and a green salad.

COOKING SCHOOL

I once made this pasta for 35 friends; the trick to making it in bulk is to use frozen corn kernels!

Shrooms 'n' Parmesan Grits

The first time George met my family, we all gathered for dinner at Crook's Corner, an institution in Chapel Hill, North Carolina, famed for shrimp 'n' grits. It was love at first sight: me, with the dish, and my mother, with George. My version features the most beautiful mix of mushrooms that I can find at the market, but you can also add shrimp to the ragu for a few minutes just before serving for a more classic version.

SERVES 2

FOR THE MUSHROOM RAGU

2 Tbsp unsalted butter

2 garlic cloves, minced

1 large shallot, minced

8 oz [230 g] mixed mushrooms, chopped into ½-in [12-mm] pieces

½ cup [120 ml] water

One 14.5-oz [415-g] can crushed tomatoes with their juice

1 Tbsp tomato paste

2 tsp red wine vinegar

2 tsp fresh thyme leaves

¾ tsp kosher salt

½ tsp smoked paprika

⅛ tsp freshly ground black pepper

Pinch of red pepper flakes

FOR THE GRITS

½ cup [70 g] grits

1½ cups [360 ml] water

½ cup [120 g] heavy cream

2 Tbsp unsalted butter

½ tsp kosher salt

⅛ tsp freshly ground black pepper

½ cup [15 g] grated Parmesan cheese, plus more for garnishing

2 Poached Eggs (page 48)

2 Tbsp fresh chopped parsley leaves

To make the mushroom ragu: In a large skillet over medium-low heat, melt 1 Tbsp of the butter. Add the garlic and shallot. Cook for 3 minutes, stirring frequently, until the shallot softens slightly. Add the mushrooms and cook for 3 to 5 minutes more, until they have released their juices and the juices evaporate. Stir in the water, crushed tomatoes, tomato paste, vinegar, thyme, salt, paprika, black pepper, and the red pepper flakes. Raise the heat to high to bring the mixture to a boil. Turn the heat to low and simmer for 20 minutes. The ragu should be about the consistency of a thick tomato pasta sauce. If thicker than that, stir in a splash of water. Start making the grits about 15 minutes before the ragu is ready.

continued

To make the grits: In a medium saucepan over high heat, stir together the grits, water, cream, butter, salt, pepper, and Parmesan cheese. Bring to a boil. Reduce to a simmer and cover the pan. Cook for about 15 minutes, stirring every 2 minutes, or until the grits absorb all liquid and thicken. If you want them thicker, continue cooking. If you want them looser, whisk in a bit of water, heavy cream, or chicken broth. They should be thick, but when you spoon them into a bowl they should spread, not hold together as a mass.

While the grits cook, make the poached eggs.

Divide the grits between two bowls. Top with about 1/3 cup [65 g] of mushroom ragu and 1 poached egg. Garnish with Parmesan cheese and fresh parsley. Enjoy immediately. Store any leftover ragu in an airtight container in the refrigerator for up to 3 days. Grits should really be enjoyed immediately or discarded.

LEFTOVERS ARE A GOOD THING

Use any leftover ragu the next morning to make No Recipe Saucy Baked Eggs (page 39).

DO YOUR THING

Substitute water, milk, or chicken broth for the heavy cream to lighten up the grits.

DO YOUR THING

Want to make it Shrooms 'n' Shrimp 'n' Grits? Add 1/2 lb [230 g] of peeled, deveined shrimp to the ragu for the last 10 minutes while the ragu is simmering over low heat.

Veggie Bibimbap

Full disclosure: Cooking this dish is a marathon. It's a fun one when you're in the mood to hang out, drink wine, listen to music, and cook together. It is *not* the right recipe for a busy weeknight. That said, the time spent cooking is completely justified by the delicious bibimbap that is the fruit of your labor. Bibimbap is a traditional Korean meal that literally translates to "mixed rice." Crispy rice is topped with an assortment of prepared veggies, which I've updated and Americanized a bit in my own version.

SERVES 4

FOR THE LEMON-MARINATED ZUCCHINI

1 large zucchini, cut lengthwise with a vegetable peeler into thin slices or spiralized

Juice of ½ lemon

¼ tsp kosher salt

FOR THE SESAME BEAN SPROUTS

1 cup [120 g] bean sprouts

1 Tbsp toasted sesame oil

¼ tsp kosher salt

FOR THE CRISPY RICE

1 cup [200 g] Japanese short-grain sushi rice or unrinsed Arborio rice

2 cups [480 ml] water

1 Tbsp toasted sesame oil

FOR THE SOY BUTTER MUSHROOMS

1 Tbsp unsalted butter

1 garlic clove, minced

8 oz [230 g] fresh mushrooms (any variety), thinly sliced

1 Tbsp soy sauce

FOR THE PEACH GOCHUJANG SAUCE

½ ripe peach, pitted and quartered (save the other half for the toppings)

½ cup [136 g] gochujang

2 tsp rice vinegar

1 Tbsp sesame oil

1 Tbsp water

FOR ADDITIONAL TOPPINGS

½ cup [50 g] drained kimchi

4 small radishes, thinly sliced

½ ripe peach, thinly sliced

2 Soft-Fried Eggs (page 47)

continued

To make the lemon-marinated zucchini: In a small bowl, toss the zucchini with the lemon juice and salt. Set aside to marinate.

To make the sesame bean sprouts: In a small bowl, toss together the bean sprouts, sesame oil, and salt. Set aside to marinate.

To make the crispy rice: In a medium saucepan with a lid, combine the rice with enough water to cover and swirl it around with your hand. Drain through a fine-mesh sieve. Return the rice to the saucepan and repeat the rinsing process at least four times, or until the water is clear when you drain it.

Return the rice to the saucepan and add the 2 cups water. Partially cover the pot and bring to a boil over high heat. Turn the heat to low, stir once, cover the pot completely, and simmer for 9 to 12 minutes, or until the rice is tender. Remove from the heat and let sit, covered, for 10 minutes. Fluff the rice with a fork and re-cover the pot for a few minutes more.

In a 12-in [30-cm] cast iron skillet over medium-high heat, warm the sesame oil. Add the cooked rice and pat it down evenly. Cook for 12 to 15 minutes until the rice forms a crispy dark brown crust.

Meanwhile, make the soy butter mushrooms: In a nonstick skillet over medium heat, melt the butter. Add the garlic, mushrooms, and soy sauce. Cook for 4 to 5 minutes, stirring frequently, until softened and browned.

To make the peach gochujang sauce: In a food processor, purée the peach, gochujang, vinegar, sesame oil, and water until smooth.

When the rice is ready, remove from the heat. In the skillet, pile the zucchini, bean sprouts, mushrooms, kimchi, radishes, and peach slices over top in separate piles around the perimeter. Place the eggs in the center. Drizzle everything with peach gochujang sauce. Serve the bibimbap straight out of the skillet, with two plates for eating.

DO YOUR THING

Sauté a bit of ground beef with sesame oil and peach gochujang sauce if you want to add meat to your bowl.

COOKING SCHOOL

The technique for cooking crispy rice is so easy and unique. Serve crispy rice straight out of the skillet with a sprinkle of chopped fresh cilantro or fresh parsley as a side dish.

MAKE IT A MEAL

Need a quicker meal tonight? Serve the soy butter mushrooms over the crispy rice. Add grilled chicken if you need protein.

Pan-Seared Scallops with Strawberry-Avocado Salsa

Want to impress your date-for-life with a restaurant-quality dish? Scallops are one of those proteins that seem *incredibly* intimidating to cook at home but, in truth, couldn't be easier to master (and show off with!). A really hot skillet is all you need to achieve perfect scallops at home. And, sure, a little butter doesn't hurt.

SERVES 2

FOR THE STRAWBERRY-AVOCADO SALSA

1 avocado, diced

½ cup [70 g] diced strawberries

¼ cup [10 g] finely chopped fresh cilantro

2 Tbsp finely chopped red onion

Juice of 1 lime

1 tsp honey

½ tsp grated peeled fresh ginger

Pinch of salt

Pinch of red pepper flakes

FOR THE PAN-SEARED SCALLOPS

1 lb [455 g] sea scallops

Pinch of salt

Pinch of freshly ground black pepper

1 Tbsp olive oil

1 Tbsp unsalted butter

To make the strawberry-avocado salsa: In a small bowl, stir together the avocado, strawberries, cilantro, red onion, lime juice, honey, ginger, salt, and red pepper flakes. Cover tightly in a glass container and refrigerate until ready to use.

To make the pan-seared scallops: Preheat a large skillet over medium-high heat for at least 3 minutes. Pat the scallops completely dry with a clean paper towel. Season with salt and pepper and drizzle with the olive oil. Add to the skillet and cook for 3 to 4 minutes, until golden brown on the first side. Flip and cook for 1 minute more. Add the butter to the pan and swirl to coat for about 1 minute more. Divide the scallops between two plates and top with strawberry-avocado salsa.

SEASONALITY

Not strawberry season? Swap in a seasonal fruit, or use frozen. Or forego the salsa altogether and, instead, add another tablespoon of butter and capers when you add the butter to the pan.

DO YOUR THING

Shrimp make a great substitution for scallops. Cook using the same technique, until opaque and pink, about 3 minutes total.

Cast Iron Pizza

Our most romantic at-home date nights are the ones when we're both in the kitchen, glasses of wine in hand, making a meal together. These cast iron pizzas are not only delicious, but also so much fun to make side by side.

Sausage and Honey Pizzas

Don't knock it till you try it—this spicy and sweet combo is unexpected but makes so much sense once you take that first bite.

MAKES TWO 10-IN [25-CM] PIZZAS

One 1-lb [455 g] store-bought pizza dough ball, halved

½ cup [120 ml] marinara sauce

1 cup [240 g] mascarpone cheese

5⅓ oz [152 g] spicy Italian ground sausage, cooked and crumbled

2 Tbsp honey

½ serrano chile, thinly sliced

2 Tbsp finely chopped fresh parsley leaves

Red pepper flakes for topping (optional)

Grated Parmesan cheese for topping (optional)

Preheat the oven to 500°F [260°C] and position a rack in the upper third of the oven.

Place a 10-in [25-cm] cast iron skillet over medium-high heat. Dust a work surface with flour and roll half the pizza dough into a 10-in [25-cm] circle. Sprinkle flour in the skillet and place the dough in it.

While the bottom of the pizza cooks, add the toppings: Spread ¼ cup [60 ml] of the marinara sauce over the dough, leaving a ½-in [12-mm] border. Distribute ½ cup [120 g] of the mascarpone cheese by dropping about 10 spoonfuls over the sauce. Spread half the cooked sausage over the top.

Once the bottom of the pizza is set and lightly browned, transfer the skillet to the oven and cook for about 10 minutes, or until the crust is golden brown.

Remove the skillet from the oven and transfer the pizza to a cutting board. Top with 1 tablespoon of the honey, half the serrano slices, and half the parsley. Serve with red pepper flakes and Parmesan cheese, if desired. Cut into slices and serve! Repeat, making a second pizza with the remaining ingredients.

SPECIAL INGREDIENT

If you have trouble finding mascarpone, use ricotta or even fresh mozzarella.

Arugula Pesto Pizza Insalata

George and I love splitting a pizza and a salad at our favorite local Italian place—and this Pesto Pizza Insalata combines both into one dish.

MAKES TWO 10-IN [25-CM] PIZZAS

FOR THE ARUGULA PESTO

2 cups [40 g] packed arugula

1 cup [30 g] grated Parmesan cheese

⅓ cup [45 g] roasted unsalted pine nuts

1 garlic clove, roughly chopped

Juice of 1 lemon

¼ tsp kosher salt

⅛ tsp freshly ground black pepper

⅔ cup [160 ml] extra-virgin olive oil

FOR THE PIZZA INSALATA

One 1-lb [455-g] store-bought pizza dough ball, halved

½ cup [40 g] shredded low-moisture part-skim mozzarella cheese

8 oz [230 g] Burrata cheese, torn into small pieces

1 cup [20 g] arugula

2 tsp fresh lemon juice

2 Tbsp grated Parmesan cheese

½ tsp kosher salt

4 oz [115 g] prosciutto, torn into strips

Preheat the oven to 500°F [260°C] and position a rack in the upper third of the oven.

To make the arugula pesto: In a food processor or blender, combine the arugula, Parmesan cheese, pine nuts, garlic, lemon juice, salt, and pepper. With the processor running, slowly add the oil. Process until smooth.

To make the pizza insalata: Place a 10-in [25-cm] cast iron skillet over medium-high heat. Dust a work surface with flour and roll half the dough into a 10-in [25-cm] circle. Sprinkle flour in the skillet and place the dough in it.

While the bottom of the pizza cooks, add the toppings: Spread ¼ cup [60 g] of the pesto over the crust, leaving a ½-in [12-mm] border. Sprinkle ¼ cup [70 g] of the mozzarella cheese and half the Burrata cheese over the pizza.

Once the bottom of the pizza is set and lightly browned, transfer the skillet to the oven and cook for about 10 minutes, or until the crust is golden brown.

Meanwhile, in a large bowl, toss the arugula with the lemon juice, Parmesan cheese, and salt.

Remove the skillet from the oven and transfer the pizza to a cutting board. Add half the prosciutto to the pizza. Cut the pizza into slices and pile half the salad on top. Repeat, making a second pizza with the remaining ingredients.

SPECIAL INGREDIENT

One container of Burrata is usually 6 to 8 oz [170 to 230 g] and contains two 3- to 4-oz [85- to 115-g] Burrata balls. If you can only find a 6-oz [170-g] container, that works, too.

Red Snapper with Leeks and Cherry Tomatoes

I love cooking my entire meal in one pan—it's so satisfying to plop one skillet straight from the oven onto the dinner table and say, "Dig in!" The leeks and cherry tomatoes melt into a rich, luscious, saucy side to accompany the crispy red snapper. I like to serve this with a loaf of good bread and nothing else, but roasted potatoes are a great side if you're hungry.

SERVES 2

2 large leeks

1 lb [455 g] skin-on red snapper fillet, cut into 2 fillets

¼ tsp kosher salt, plus more as needed

¼ tsp freshly ground black pepper, plus more as needed

1 Tbsp plus 1½ tsp olive oil

4 garlic cloves, thinly sliced

1 pint [300 g] cherry tomatoes

2 Tbsp white wine vinegar

1 Tbsp unsalted butter

Maldon sea salt

2 Tbsp chopped fresh herbs, such as basil, parsley, or cilantro

Preheat the oven to 350°F [180°C].

To prepare the leeks, cut off the tough, dark green upper leaves, trim the roots, and halve the leeks vertically. Run them under cold water to clean very thoroughly. The leaves typically are very sandy. Thinly slice into half-moons. Set aside.

Heat a 10-in [25-cm] cast iron skillet over medium-high heat for at least 4 minutes. Pat the snapper dry with paper towels. Season with the kosher salt and pepper. Coat the skin side with the 1½ tsp of the olive oil. Place the snapper fillets, skin-side down, into the pan. Using a spatula, press the fish into the skillet for 10 seconds. Cook for 3 to 4 minutes, or until deep golden brown and crispy. Transfer to a holding plate, skin-side up.

Lower the heat under the skillet to medium and warm the remaining 1 Tbsp olive oil. Add the leeks, garlic, and tomatoes and cook for 7 to 10 minutes, until the tomatoes start to soften and release their juices. Stir in the vinegar and butter, taste, and season with more kosher salt and pepper, as needed. Remove the skillet from the heat.

Place the snapper, skin-side up, on top of the tomato mixture and transfer the skillet to the oven. Cook for 8 to 10 minutes, or until the fish flakes easily when prodded with a fork. Set aside to let rest for several minutes. Garnish with sea salt and fresh herbs. Enjoy immediately.

LEFTOVERS ARE A GOOD THING

If you have leftovers, remove the skin from the fish before refrigerating, as it will become soggy and unappealing.

DO YOUR THING

Any semi-firm white fish will work in this recipe. If you have a fish without skin, skip the skin-searing step and just put the raw fish on top of the sautéed leeks and tomatoes. Cook for a couple of minutes longer in the oven.

COOKING SCHOOL

When put into a hot pan, fish fillets immediately curl, which leads to crispy middles and soggy sides. Pressing the fish into the skillet with the spatula helps the skin adhere to the pan and crisp up all over.

Crispy Chicken Thighs with Shallots and Nectarines

Bone-in, skin-on chicken thighs are an imperfect cook's best weapon. Where chicken breasts are guaranteed to dry out after a few too many minutes in the oven, chicken thighs stand the test of too much time—they're incredibly forgiving and flavorful. If nectarines are out of season, you can always swap in seasonal fruit, like apples (pictured here).

SERVES 2 TO 4

4 large (about 2 lb [910 g]) bone-in, skin-on chicken thighs

½ tsp kosher salt

¼ tsp freshly ground black pepper

1 Tbsp olive oil

3 shallots, thinly sliced

2 nectarines, each cut into 8 pieces

6 fresh thyme sprigs

1 cup [240 ml] chicken broth

3 Tbsp fresh lemon juice (from about 2 lemons)

1 Tbsp unsalted butter

Preheat the oven to 450°F [230°C].

Pat the chicken thighs dry with a paper towel, and season with the salt and pepper. If the bottoms of the chicken thighs have skin on them, use kitchen shears to remove it.

In your largest ovenproof skillet over medium-high heat, warm the olive oil. When it is very hot and shimmering, place the chicken thighs, skin-side down, in the skillet. Cook for 10 to 12 minutes, until the skin is deep golden brown and crispy. Transfer the chicken to a plate. Pour off all but 1 Tbsp chicken fat, and add the shallots and nectarines to the skillet. Lower the heat to medium and sauté until the shallots begin to soften, about 3 minutes. Remove the skillet from the heat, smooth the nectarines into an even layer, and scatter the thyme sprigs over the top.

Return the chicken to the pan, skin-side up. Nestle them into the nectarines as much as possible without covering the skin. Carefully pour in the chicken broth and lemon juice, making sure it doesn't submerge the chicken skin at all; you want the skin completely exposed. Transfer the skillet to the oven and cook for 30 minutes, or until an instant-read thermometer registers an internal temperature of 165°F [75°C].

Remove the skillet from the oven and transfer the chicken to a holding plate. Pluck out the thyme and discard it. Place the skillet over high heat and cook for 8 to 10 minutes, until the sauce is reduced by about half and coats the back of a spoon. Stir in the butter and return the thighs to the pan to keep warm over low heat until you're ready to serve.

Spatchcocked Chicken with the Best Ever Green Sauce

Aside from being a funny word, spatchcocking is, by far, the most dependable way to ensure even cooking when making a whole chicken at home (that is, without the aid of a rotisserie oven). This green sauce is like a vegan green goddess dressing—the oil emulsifies the herbs and jalapeño chile into a smooth, completely addictive sauce.

SERVES 4 TO 6

FOR THE CHICKEN	FOR THE BEST EVER GREEN SAUCE
One 4-lb whole organic chicken	⅓ cup packed cilantro leaves
2 tsp dried oregano	¼ cup packed parsley leaves
1 tsp ground cumin	2 scallions, cut into 3-inch pieces
1 tsp smoked paprika	2 garlic cloves
1 tsp garlic powder	1 jalapeño chile, seeded
½ tsp chili powder	¼ cup olive oil
½ tsp kosher salt	3 tablespoons white wine vinegar
⅛ tsp cayenne pepper	1 teaspoon kosher salt
Olive oil for cooking	½ teaspoon freshly ground black pepper

Spatchcock the chicken: Place the bird breast-side down on a work surface and pat it dry with a paper towel. Use sharp kitchen shears or a chef's knife to remove the entire backbone of the bird. Flip the chicken over and press down on the breastbone to break it and flatten it.

To make the chicken: In a small bowl, mix together the oregano, cumin, paprika, garlic powder, chili powder, salt, and cayenne pepper. Rub the spice mixture all over the chicken and refrigerate,

uncovered, for at least 1 hour, but preferably 12 hours. Remove the chicken from the refrigerator at least 1 hour before cooking.

Preheat the oven to 425°F [220°C].

Heat your largest ovenproof skillet (preferably cast iron) over medium-high heat. Add enough olive oil to coat the bottom of the skillet, and heat it for 1 to 2 minutes, until it shimmers. Place the chicken, skin-side down, in the skillet and cook for 8 to 10 minutes, until deep golden brown. Rotate the pan halfway through the cooking time to help ensure even cooking. Flip the chicken, and place the skillet in the oven. Cook for 40 to 45 minutes, until golden brown and crisp all over, and an instant-read thermometer registers 165°F [75°C].

Transfer the chicken to a clean cutting board and let rest for 10 to 15 minutes before carving.

To make the best ever green sauce: In a blender, blend the cilantro, parsley, scallions, garlic, jalapeño chile, olive oil, vinegar, salt, and black pepper until smooth.

To serve, remove the breast meat from the chicken and cut it into thick slices. Use a sharp knife to cut the wings, thighs, and legs into separate pieces. Serve with the sauce.

DO YOUR THING

Rub fresh rosemary, lemon zest, salt, and pepper on the chicken and serve with a wine sauce. Follow the recipe for the Cast Iron T-Bone with Red Wine Sauce (page 179), but use white wine instead of red and add a splash of heavy cream.

MAKE IT A MEAL

Serve the chicken with Roasted Cabbage with Brown Butter Bread Crumbs (page 231). You can roast the chicken and cabbage at the same time to make things easy.

Cast Iron T-Bone with Red Wine Sauce

When there's cause to celebrate, like a birthday or anniversary, we like to cook really nice (read: expensive) steaks in a cast iron skillet. Cooking in cast iron allows much more precise heat regulation than grilling, which is important when you've spent a decent chunk of change on good meat. Plus, collecting all the steak's juices in the skillet makes for one hell of a pan sauce, which comes together while the steak rests.

SERVES 2

One 2-in- [5-cm-] thick Porterhouse steak (about 2 lb [910 g])

½ tsp kosher salt

¼ tsp freshly ground black pepper

1 Tbsp olive oil

3 Tbsp unsalted butter

3 fresh thyme sprigs

1 tsp Dijon mustard

½ cup [120 ml] red wine

Season the steak with the salt and pepper and let it come to room temperature for at least 30 minutes before cooking.

Preheat the broiler.

In a large cast iron skillet over medium-high heat, warm the olive oil until shimmery and very hot. Add the steak and cook for 3 to 4 minutes, or until a dark golden-brown crust forms. Working quickly, turn off the heat, flip the steak, and add 1 Tbsp of the butter and the thyme to the pan. Swirl it around until it melts and use a spoon to baste the steak with the melted butter. Transfer the skillet to the highest rack in your oven and broil for 4 minutes for a medium-rare steak. Return the skillet to the stove top and transfer the steak to a cutting board.

While the steak rests, return the skillet to medium heat and whisk in the mustard and red wine, scraping up all the browned bits from the bottom of the pan.

Simmer for 5 to 7 minutes, until the sauce reduces by about half. Whisk in the remaining 2 Tbsp of the butter and remove the skillet from the heat. Taste and season with salt and pepper.

Cut the steak off the bone into two large pieces. Cut perpendicular to the bone into 1-in- [2.5-cm-] thick pieces. Serve immediately with the red wine sauce spooned over.

SPECIAL INGREDIENT

When I use wine in a recipe, I use whatever wine I'm drinking with dinner, as long as it's under $20.

COOKING SCHOOL

Giving your steak (or any meat) time to "rest" after cooking is a crucial, oft-forgotten step. Meat loses a lot less juice when sliced if given time to rest after cooking, so resting helps make it juicier and more tender.

Beer-Braised Beef with Classic Mashed Potatoes

This is a good old-fashioned, stick-to-your-bones, like-mama-used-to-make-it, pot roast. An incredibly cheap cut of meat (beef chuck), which can be a savior to newlyweds' budgets, transforms into a supple, melt-in-your-mouth dish after a long, slow braise in a bath of stout beer and aromatics.

SERVES 4

FOR THE BEER-BRAISED BEEF

One 1-lb [455-g] whole chuck roast, cut into 2-in [5-cm] steaks

1½ tsp kosher salt

½ tsp freshly ground black pepper

1 Tbsp grapeseed oil

4 garlic cloves, roughly chopped

1 large yellow onion, cut into ¼-in- [6-mm-] thick slices

2 large carrots, cut into ½-in [12-mm] cubes

One 12-oz [360-ml] bottle stout beer

2 cups [480 ml] beef broth

1 bay leaf

FOR THE CLASSIC MASHED POTATOES

1 lb [455 g] Yukon Gold potatoes, peeled and quartered

½ cup [120 ml] whole milk or heavy cream

1 Tbsp unsalted butter

½ tsp kosher salt

⅛ tsp freshly ground black pepper

Preheat the oven to 350°F [180°C].

To make the beer-braised beef: Pat the meat completely dry with paper towels. Season with 1 tsp of the salt and the ½ tsp pepper.

In a small (about 3½-qt [3.3-L]) Dutch oven over medium-high heat, warm the grapeseed oil. Sear the meat for 3 to 4 minutes per side. Transfer the seared meat to a holding plate. Lower the heat to medium. Add the garlic, onion, and carrots and cook for 4 to 5 minutes, until the vegetables soften slightly. Pour in the beer and broth and add the bay leaf. Raise the heat to high and bring to a boil. Stir up any

browned bits that might be stuck to the bottom of the pan. Return the beef and any accumulated juices to the pot. Cover the pot and transfer to the oven.

Cook for 2½ to 3 hours, until the meat is very tender but you can still lift it out of the pot without it falling apart. Transfer the meat to a cutting board and return the Dutch oven to high heat on the stove top for 10 minutes to reduce the sauce slightly.

To make the classic mashed potatoes: Bring a large pot of salted water to a boil over high heat. Add the potatoes and boil for 20 minutes, or until they fall apart when pierced with a fork.

Meanwhile, in a small saucepan over medium-low heat, warm the milk and melt the butter with it. Drain the potatoes and transfer to a medium bowl. Smash and stir vigorously with a fork to break them apart. Stir in the warmed milk-butter mixture and season with salt and pepper.

To serve, divide the potatoes between two bowls and top with meat and sauce.

TOOL TIP

If you're into slow cookers, this is a great recipe for that cooking method. Cook for about 6 hours on low heat.

DO YOUR THING

Substitute 1½ cups [360 ml] of red wine for the beer for a more classic red wine–braised beef similar to beef bourguignon.

BUY SMART

Ask the butcher to cut a 1-lb [455-g] cut of chuck roast for you. If he won't, buy a piece (usually 3 lb [1.4 kg]), cut it into thirds, and freeze the rest.

Korean Sliced Beef

When less expensive cuts of meat are marinated and dressed up right, they can be just as special as the most expensive T-bone your butcher has to offer. Here, inexpensive flat iron steak gets a 24-hour Korean flavor bath before being grilled and served simply with steamed white rice and kimchi.

SERVES 4

⅓ cup [91 g] gochujang

4 garlic cloves

One 2-in [5-cm] piece fresh peeled ginger

2 Tbsp light brown sugar

2 Tbsp rice vinegar

2 Tbsp soy sauce

1 Tbsp fish sauce

⅓ cup [80 ml] grapeseed oil

2 Tbsp water

½ bunch fresh cilantro leaves and stems, plus more leaves for garnishing

One 1½- to 2-lb [680- to 910-g] flat iron steak

Olive oil for the steak

Steamed white rice and kimchi for serving

In a blender, combine the gochujang, garlic, ginger, brown sugar, vinegar, soy sauce, fish sauce, grapeseed oil, cilantro, and the water. Blend on high speed until smooth. Reserve ⅓ cup [80 ml] of the marinade and pour the remaining marinade into a large resealable plastic bag. Add the steak, seal the bag, and lay it flat in your refrigerator for at least 2 hours, but preferably 12 to 24 hours.

Remove the steak from the refrigerator 30 minutes before you're ready to cook and let it come to room temperature.

Preheat an outdoor grill to medium-high heat (see Tool Tip).

Scrape the marinade off the steak and drizzle it generously with olive oil. For medium-rare, cook the steak for 6 minutes on the first side, flip, and cook for 4 minutes more. Let the steak rest for 5 to 10 minutes

before slicing. Thinly slice against the grain (see Cooking School, page 114), and scatter cilantro leaves over the top. Serve with rice, kimchi, and reserved marinade as a sauce on the side.

TOOL TIP

If you don't have an outdoor grill, sear both sides of the steak in a skillet over high heat and transfer to a 500°F [260°C] oven to finish cooking, as with the Cast Iron T-Bone with Red Wine Sauce (page 179).

MAKE IT A MEAL

To complete your Korean dinner, serve with white rice, kimchi, and a few of the Veggie Bibimbap (page 165) components, such as the Soy Butter Mushrooms (page 165). Or, go for a healthier starch and serve with baked sweet potatoes.

Fig-Glazed Pork Belly

Pork belly is another one of those proteins that seems to be relegated to restaurants but is incredibly simple to cook perfectly at home. This tender, sweet, and sticky pork belly will make you and your love wonder why you ever go out to eat at all!

SERVES 4

1½ to 2 lb [680 to 910 g] pork belly

½ tsp kosher salt

¼ cup [80 g] fig jam

2 Tbsp Dijon mustard

½ cup [120 ml] plus 1 Tbsp apple cider vinegar

4 garlic cloves, smashed

2 bay leaves

½ cup [120 ml] chicken broth, plus more as needed

Preheat the oven to 400°F [200°C].

Rinse the pork belly under cold running water and pat completely dry with paper towels. Use a fork to poke hundreds of holes all over the skin (the thick white layer). Be sure to penetrate the skin only, not down into the meat. Season with the salt.

In a small saucepan over medium heat, combine the fig jam, mustard, and the 1 Tbsp of apple cider vinegar. Cook for about 5 minutes, stirring frequently so it doesn't scorch, until thickened and slightly reduced. Remove from the heat.

Heat a large cast iron skillet over medium-high heat for at least 3 minutes until very hot. (If the pork belly doesn't fit in your largest cast iron skillet, use any ovenproof skillet that it will fit in, preferably nonstick.) Sear the pork belly, skin-side down, for 4 to 5 minutes, until golden brown and crispy. Remove the skillet from the heat and flip the pork belly. Carefully pour the fig glaze over the crispy pork belly skin, trying not to let it run off the sides. Place the garlic cloves and bay leaves around the pork and pour the remaining ½ cup [120 ml] apple cider vinegar and the broth around—not over!—the pork belly.

Roast the pork belly for about 10 minutes, until it starts to form a crust on top. Turn the temperature down to 225°F [110°C] and roast for 3 hours, checking every now and then to make sure there's still ½ in [12 mm] of liquid surrounding the pork. If there isn't, pour in more broth.

Transfer the pork belly to a cutting board and let rest for at least 10 minutes. Use a serrated knife to cut the belly into ½-in- [12-mm-] thick slices.

MAKE AHEAD

Make the pork belly up to 3 days in advance. Let it cool completely and wrap tightly in plastic wrap. When it's time to serve, cut it into slices ½ in [12 mm] thick and warm in a 300°F [150°C] oven for about 10 minutes. Cutting it cold creates neater slices.

DO YOUR THING

No fig jam? Use apricot, blueberry, or whatever you have. Or, make a paste with equal parts Dijon mustard and brown sugar instead.

Juiciest Pork Tenderloin

Pork tenderloin is a wonderful, inexpensive, and lean cut of meat, but with one wrong turn it can become overcooked and dry, so it often gets a bad reputation. We found a completely foolproof method by roasting it in a flavorful bath.

SERVES 4

1 lb [455 g] pork tenderloin

½ tsp kosher salt

½ tsp freshly cracked black pepper

1 Tbsp olive oil

2 cups [480 ml] chicken broth

1 cup [240 ml] apple cider vinegar

2 Tbsp Dijon mustard

2 Tbsp maple syrup

1 large fennel bulb, trimmed and cut into ¼-in-by-1-in [6-mm-by-2.5-cm] slices

½ cup [70 g] dried cherries

½ cup [80 g] pitted Kalamata olives

2 fresh rosemary sprigs

4 fresh thyme sprigs

Preheat the oven to 325°F [165°C].

Remove the meat from the refrigerator 30 minutes before cooking. Season with the salt and pepper.

In a 12-in [30-cm] ovenproof skillet over medium-high heat, warm the olive oil. Sear the pork tenderloin for about 2 minutes per side, on all 4 sides, until golden brown all over. Transfer the tenderloin to a plate. Return the skillet to medium-high heat and pour in the broth, vinegar, mustard, and maple syrup. Whisk until smooth, scraping up any browned bits. Return the tenderloin to the skillet and scatter the fennel, cherries, olives, rosemary, and thyme around either side.

Place the skillet in the oven and cook for 30 to 45 minutes, until the internal temperature registers 145°F [65°C]. Transfer the tenderloin to a cutting board to rest.

Place the skillet over high heat for 8 to 10 minutes to reduce the sauce by half. Turn off the heat; remove and discard the rosemary and thyme sprigs. Cut the tenderloin into ½-in [12-mm] slices and arrange on a small platter. Use a slotted spoon to place fennel, cherries, and olives over the top. Serve immediately with the reduced sauce on the side.

DO YOUR THING

You can use cauliflower or sweet potatoes instead of fennel, and golden raisins or dried figs in place of the cherries.

COOKING SCHOOL

Recently, the USDA's standard safe temperature recommendation for cooked pork was lowered from 160°F [70°C] to 145°F [65°C]. Oh what a different those few degrees make to the juiciness of a pork tenderloin!

Despite living in *shockingly* tiny spaces for the first many years of our marriage, George and I have always loved hosting dinner parties for our friends and family. We have friends over for dinner at least twice a week because, on our military-turned-graduate-school budget, cooking for four to six people has proven over and over to be cheaper than dining out. Am I cooking $20-per-lb [455 g] salmon for six people? No way. When I cook for friends, I buy inexpensive cuts of meat and take really good care of them—like slow-roasting pork for 7 hours for my Chipotle Carnitas Tacos (page 206), or a flavorful, overnight marinade as in my Vietnamese Chicken Skewers with Grilled Scallions (page 195).

These recipes will make entertaining affordable and easy. They're forgiving—if you leave the Harissa Braised Short Ribs (page 205) in the oven for an extra 30 minutes because someone's (not saying who!) notoriously late best friend shows up even later than you anticipated—no sweat. Chicken and Bok Choy Khao Soi (page 190) and Beef Chili with All the Fixin's (page 201) can sit on the back burner over low heat for hours until all your guests finally arrive. These recipes allow you to focus on your guests, rather than what's on the stove, because the people gathered around your table are the most important.

Mom's Mac and Cheese

My mom never works from a recipe, so when I asked her for her famous mac and cheese recipe, she just laughed. I had to have her recipe in this book, so I spent an afternoon watching her make it—stopping her to measure each ingredient as she flailed around the kitchen. We laughed so hard that day, me screaming at her to slow down, her screaming at me to hurry up. That day spent in my childhood kitchen, cooking with my mom to get this recipe down on paper might be my greatest triumph of this entire book. Your loved ones' joy when you cook it for them might just become your greatest kitchen triumph, too.

SERVES 6 TO 8

6 Tbsp [85 g] unsalted butter, plus more for the baking dish

1 lb [455 g] rotini noodles

¼ cup [35 g] all-purpose flour

3½ cups [840 ml] whole milk

8 oz [230 g] sharp white Cheddar cheese, shredded

8 oz [230 g] Havarti cheese, shredded

8 oz [230 g] Monterey Jack cheese, shredded

1¼ tsp kosher salt

2 tsp garlic powder

2 tsp dry mustard

1 cup [60 g] panko bread crumbs

1 Tbsp fresh thyme leaves

Preheat the oven to 350°F [180°C]. Butter a 4-qt [3.8-L] baking dish.

Cook the noodles for about 7 minutes until al dente. In a colander, drain and rinse.

In a large saucepan over medium heat, melt 4 Tbsp [60 g] of the butter. Sprinkle the flour over and whisk constantly, about 1 minute. Slowly whisk in the milk, 1/2 cup [120 ml] at a time, until the flour dissolves. Raise the heat to high and bring the mixture to a boil. Lower the heat to maintain a simmer and whisk frequently until the sauce thickens, 8 to 10 minutes. The sauce should not look or feel grainy when you rub it between your fingers.

Whisk the cheeses into the sauce 1 cup [80 g] at a time, fully incorporating each cup before adding the next. Whisk in 1 tsp of the salt, 1½ tsp of the garlic powder, and the dry mustard.

Add the noodles to the sauce, toss to combine, and transfer to the prepared dish.

In a medium nonstick skillet over medium heat, melt the remaining 2 Tbsp of butter. Stir in the bread crumbs, remaining ¼ tsp salt, and remaining ½ tsp garlic powder. Cook for 3 to 4 minutes, stirring frequently, until light golden brown. Remove from the heat, stir in the thyme, and scatter over the noodles. Transfer the baking dish to the oven and bake for 25 to 30 minutes, until the cheese is bubbling and the bread crumbs are golden brown. Cool for several minutes before serving.

Chicken and Bok Choy Khao Soi (Thai Chicken Noodle Soup)

The winding dirt roads, elephant sanctuaries, ancient temples, and hidden waterfalls are what make Chiang Mai, a town in Northern Thailand, a beloved tourist destination. But what keeps us coming back is the unbelievably unique Northern Thai cuisine, a far cry from the spring rolls and pad Thai found in most Thai restaurants in the United States. Many classic Northern Thai dishes are punchy, pungent, and often potent beyond my taste buds' liking—but khao soi has become a hit among many Westerners, including George and me. Basically a curried chicken noodle soup, khao soi boasts a perfect balance of acidity and creaminess and packs a major umami punch thanks to a hefty pour of fish sauce. My version is as close to the real thing as you can get without having to spend the day hunting for obscure Asian ingredients—curry paste and fish sauce are the only wild cards, but they're available in most major grocery stores. We love setting up a khao soi buffet with noodles, the soup, and all the toppings and letting our dinner guests go wild.

SERVES 4

1 Tbsp grapeseed oil or other neutral oil

1 bunch fresh cilantro, stems cut off and minced; leaves reserved for garnishing

2 to 3 Tbsp yellow or red curry paste

2 garlic cloves, minced

1 small shallot, minced

One 1-in [2.5 cm] piece peeled fresh ginger, minced

3 cups [720 ml] chicken broth

Two 14-oz [420-ml] cans unsweetened coconut milk

1 lb [455 g] boneless, skinless chicken thighs

2 large heads bok choy

1 lb [455 g] egg noodles, cooked according to the package directions

3 Tbsp fish sauce

1 Tbsp soy sauce

1 Tbsp light brown sugar

Juice of 1 lime

FOR THE TOPPINGS

Sriracha, sliced scallions, chopped fresh cilantro, Pickled Red Onions (page 82), lime wedges, crunchy chow mein noodles

continued

In a large heavy pot over medium heat, warm the oil. Add the minced cilantro stems, curry paste (use 3 Tbsp if you like things spicy), garlic, shallot, and ginger. Cook for 4 minutes, stirring constantly. The paste will stick to the bottom of your pot; that's OK. Add 1 cup [240 ml] of the chicken broth and remove from the heat. Use a wooden spoon to stir, scraping up any paste that stuck to the bottom of the pot. Transfer the broth mixture to a high-powered blender and blend for 30 seconds.

Pour the broth mixture back into the pot and stir in the remaining 2 cups [480 ml] broth and the coconut milk. Raise the heat to high and bring to a boil. Turn the heat to low, add the chicken and simmer for 30 minutes, covered. Transfer the chicken to a large plate and shred it.

While the chicken cooks, prepare the bok choy by pulling each leaf apart and rinsing under cold water (they can be very dirty inside; sometimes I even spin the leaves in a salad spinner). Cut each leaf from the base to tip into long, ¼-in- [6-mm-] thick strips. Set aside.

Cook your noodles so they finish cooking just before your chicken finishes. (For instance, if your noodles take 8 minutes to cook, put them in the pot when the chicken has been cooking for about 20 minutes and still has 10 minutes left to cook.) Drain and rinse with water so they don't clump together.

To the soup, still over low heat, stir in the fish sauce, soy sauce, light brown sugar, lime juice, shredded chicken, and bok choy strips. The soup is ready as soon as the bok choy wilts, about 2 minutes.

Divide the noodles and soup among bowls and serve with your desired toppings: Sriracha, scallions, cilantro, pickled red onions, lime wedges, or crunchy chow mein noodles.

LEFTOVERS ARE A GOOD THING

These leftovers are wonderful; just keep the noodles and the soup separate until you're ready to reheat. Cover the noodles with a damp paper towel in an airtight container so they don't harden.

MAKE AHEAD

The entire soup can be made ahead and reheated when you're ready to serve. Just stir in the bok choy at the very last minute.

DO YOUR THING

Traditional khao soi is made using a freshly ground yellow curry paste, but restaurants and stands in Chiang Mai serve it made with every type of curry paste imaginable. Use your favorite; just adjust the amount based on the heat level. If fish sauce scares you, omit it but be sure to season with salt instead.

Leftover Thanksgiving Turkey Curry

Thanksgiving leftovers are perhaps the most sacred leftovers of all. Though the classic turkey leftover sandwich is a given for lunch, no one's going to say no to gathering around the table again to enjoy a warm bowl of turkey curry for dinner one night during Thanksgiving weekend.

SERVES 4

2 cups [400 g] uncooked brown rice

1 Tbsp grapeseed oil

1 Tbsp minced peeled fresh ginger

2 garlic cloves, minced

1 small yellow onion, chopped

2 Tbsp red curry paste

One 14.5-oz [415-g] can crushed tomatoes

1 cup [240 ml] canned coconut milk

½ cup [120 ml] water

1 Tbsp fish sauce

1 tablespoon brown sugar

1 tsp kosher salt

1 small butternut squash, cut into 1-in [2.5-cm] cubes

2 cups [30 g] chopped kale

2 cups [280 g] chopped leftover turkey

¼ cup [5 g] chiffonade fresh basil leaves

1 lime, cut into 4 wedges

Cook the brown rice (see Quick Cooking Reference Guide, page 263).

In a large heavy-bottomed pot (preferably a Dutch oven) over medium heat, heat the oil for several minutes until it shimmers. Add the ginger, garlic, and onion. Cook for 5 to 7 minutes, stirring often, until the onion is translucent. Add the curry paste and stir it in for about 30 seconds. It will stick to the bottom of the pot; that's OK.

Stir in the tomatoes, coconut milk, water, and the fish sauce. Raise the heat to high and bring the mixture to a boil.

Lower the heat to medium, add the brown sugar, salt, and butternut squash, and stir to cover with liquid. Cover the pot and cook for 12 to 15 minutes, until the squash is fork-tender. Remove the lid and stir in the kale and turkey. Cook for 2 to 3 minutes, until the turkey is warmed through and the kale is wilted. Divide the rice and curry among four bowls, garnish with fresh basil, and serve with a lime wedge.

LEFTOVERS ARE A GOOD THING

This recipe is awesome with any leftover protein: shrimp, beef, grilled or pulled chicken, etc. Just remember to toss it in at the very end just to warm it through; you don't want to continue cooking it or it will get over-cooked and tough.

Chicken Skewers

Skewers are so versatile: Use mini skewers to turn these recipes into an appetizer, add vegetables to the skewer for a backyard barbecue, or serve them with a fork and knife for a sit-down meal! The Yogurt-Marinated Chicken Skewers have Mediterranean flavors. The Vietnamese version is inspired by their incredible street food.

Yogurt-Marinated Chicken Skewers with Yogurt Sauce

The lactic acid in yogurt tenderizes the chicken to juicy perfection. They're great on their own or with pita bread and lots of toppings to let your guests build their own sandwiches.

SERVES 4 TO 6

1½ cups [360 g] plain yogurt

Zest and juice of 1 lemon

1 tsp ground cumin

1 tsp garlic powder

½ tsp kosher salt

⅛ tsp freshly ground black pepper

⅛ tsp cayenne pepper

1½ lb [680 g] boneless, skinless chicken breasts, cut lengthwise into ¼-in- [6-mm-] thick strips

4 pita breads

1 cup [120 g] cucumber slices

1 avocado, sliced

Maldon sea salt

Fresh chopped herbs, sliced tomatoes, thinly sliced red onion, lemon wedges for serving (optional)

In a large bowl, whisk the yogurt, lemon zest and juice, cumin, garlic powder, kosher salt, black pepper, and cayenne pepper. Reserve ½ cup [120 g] of the yogurt mixture in a small bowl for later use as a sauce. Stir the chicken into the large bowl of yogurt marinade to coat. Cover with plastic wrap, refrigerate, and marinate for at least 1 hour, and up to 24 hours.

Preheat a grill or a stove-top grill pan to medium-high heat

Shake off as much marinade as possible from the chicken and thread it loosely onto wooden skewers that have been soaked in water, so it's stretched out, not bunched tightly. Alternatively, use metal skewers— no soaking required!

Oil the grill and grill the skewers for 3 minutes. Flip and cook for 3 to 4 minutes more, or until an instant-read thermometer registers 165°F [75°C]. If using a grill pan, you'll need 5 to 7 minutes per side to cook the chicken through. Grill the pita for a couple of minutes to lightly toast and warm through.

Transfer the chicken to a large serving platter along with the reserved yogurt sauce, grilled pita, cucumber slices, avocado slices, sea salt, fresh chopped herbs, sliced tomatoes, thinly sliced red onion, and lemon wedges (if you like) and any other desired accompaniments. Encourage your eaters to pull their chicken off the skewer and make mini pita bites with pita triangles, toppings, and yogurt sauce.

Vietnamese Chicken Skewers with Grilled Scallions

These sweet and savory skewers are inspired by the ones sold roadside all over Vietnam.

SERVES 4 TO 6

½ cup [100 g] sugar	1 Tbsp sambal oelek
⅓ cup [80 ml] fish sauce	5 garlic cloves, grated
⅓ cup [80 ml] warm water	1½ lb [680 g] boneless, skinless chicken breasts, cut lengthwise into ¼-in- [6-mm-] thick strips
¼ cup [60 ml] plus 2 tsp grapeseed oil or other neutral oil	
2 Tbsp toasted sesame oil	2 bunches scallions, stems trimmed
2 Tbsp rice vinegar	¼ cup [3 g] torn fresh mint leaves

In a large bowl, whisk the sugar, fish sauce, water, 1/4 cup [60 ml] of the grapeseed oil, sesame oil, vinegar, sambal oelek, and garlic. Transfer ½ cup [120 ml] of the marinade to a small bowl for later use as a sauce. Stir the chicken into the marinade, cover with plastic wrap, and refrigerate for at least 3 hours, but preferably 24 hours.

Preheat a grill to medium-high heat.

Thread the chicken loosely onto wooden skewers that have been soaked in water, so it's stretched out, not bunched tightly. Alternatively, use metal skewers—no soaking required! Grill the chicken for 3 minutes, flip, and cook for 3 to 4 minutes more, or until an instant-read thermometer registers 165°F [75°C].

In a small bowl, toss the scallions with the remaining 2 tsp grapeseed oil. Grill for 4 to 5 minutes while the chicken cooks, or until soft and charred. Transfer the chicken and scallions to a serving platter, brush the chicken with the reserved marinade, scatter fresh mint over the top, and serve the remaining marinade alongside as dipping sauce.

Baked Meatballs

This is the recipe to pull out when your meat-loving friends are headed over for dinner. The generous amount of ricotta helps keep the meatballs moist, and the sauce—succulent and easy as can be—tastes like your Italian nona made it fresh that morning. This recipe makes a *lot* of meatballs. Make your meatballs smaller and serve with pasta so everyone gets more, or make them giant so everyone gets only one. Or, halve the recipe (use one egg) to feed four. Don't forget to shower everyone's meatballs with Parmesan cheese—best done at the last minute at the dinner table for effect.

SERVES 8 TO 10

FOR THE TOMATO SAUCE

2 Tbsp olive oil

2 Tbsp tomato paste

2 tsp kosher salt

1 garlic clove, roughly chopped

1 tsp dried oregano

Two 28-oz [800-g] cans whole tomatoes and their juices

FOR THE MEATBALLS

3 large eggs

1 lb [455 g] 85% lean ground beef

1 lb [455 g] ground pork

½ cup [120 g] ricotta cheese

½ cup [30 g] panko bread crumbs

¼ cup [10 g] finely chopped fresh parsley, plus more for garnishing

2 garlic cloves, grated

2 tsp dried oregano

2 tsp kosher salt

¼ tsp red pepper flakes

2 Tbsp olive oil

Parmesan cheese for showering

Preheat the oven to 425°F [220°C]. Spray a 9-by-13-in [23-by-33-cm] baking dish with nonstick cooking spray.

To make the tomato sauce: In a blender, combine the olive oil, tomato paste, salt, garlic, oregano, and tomatoes. Blend on high speed until combined but still slightly chunky.

To make the meatballs: In a large bowl, lightly whisk the eggs. Add the ground beef, ground pork, ricotta cheese, bread crumbs, parsley, garlic, oregano, salt, and red pepper flakes. Use clean hands to combine. The mixture will be pretty wet and sticky; wet your hands to prevent the meat mixture from sticking to them when rolling the meatballs. Form the meat mixture into ¼-cup-size [115-g] meatballs. You should get about 18 large meatballs. Place the meatballs in the prepared baking dish and drizzle with olive oil.

Bake the meatballs for 20 minutes. Remove from the oven, carefully pour off any excess fat, and top with the tomato sauce. Use a spatula to roll the meatballs around a bit and make sure the sauce gets down between all of them. Lower the oven temperature to 350°F [180°C] and continue cooking for 30 minutes more.

Garnish with parsley and freshly grated Parmesan cheese and serve immediately.

LEFTOVERS ARE A GOOD THING

Freeze any leftover meatballs with the sauce in an air-tight container for a quick dinner another night.

MAKE AHEAD

The meatballs can be made ahead; just reduce the final cooking time to 15 minutes, cool completely, and refrigerate. Reheat at 350°F [180°C] for 20 to 30 minutes, until warmed through. You can keep the meatballs warm in a 200°F [95°C] oven for up to 1 hour until you're ready to serve.

DO YOUR THING

If you're short on time, forego making the tomato sauce. Just pour diced canned tomatoes over the meatballs and sprinkle salt, oregano, and garlic powder on top. Use ground turkey in place of ground beef for a lighter meatball.

MAKE IT A MEAL

Serve with spaghetti for a traditional spaghetti-and-meatballs meal, or start with a simple salad and serve the meatballs by themselves with extra Parmesan cheese and crusty bread for scooping. Or, serve as meatball sliders on mini buns!

Beef Chili with All the Fixin's

A big pot of chili is the perfect food for "drop by" guests—like when your parents are in town, but there's no set mealtime and they'll show up whenever. You can also easily double or triple this recipe for a crowd—just use a big pot and be sure to serve it with all the fixin's!

SERVES 4 TO 6

2 poblano chiles

1 canned chipotle chile in adobo sauce

1 qt [960 ml] low-sodium chicken broth

2 Tbsp grapeseed oil

1½ lb [680 g] boneless beef chuck, cut into ½-in [12-mm] cubes

Kosher salt

Freshly ground black pepper

1 large yellow onion, finely chopped

4 garlic cloves, finely chopped

2 tsp ground cumin

1 tsp dried oregano

½ tsp chili powder

One 14-oz [400-g] can whole tomatoes and their juices

One 12-oz [340-g] can black beans, drained and rinsed

FOR THE FIXIN'S BAR

Sour cream, corn chips or tortilla chips, chopped fresh cilantro, diced and seeded jalapeño chile, diced avocado

Over high heat on a gas stove-top burner, cook the poblano chiles, skewered on a fork, on all sides until heavily charred, about 4 minutes per side. If you don't have a gas stove, cook the poblanos under the broiler. Scrape off a bit of the char, remove the seeds and stems, and transfer the poblano flesh and the chipotle chile to a blender. Add the broth and blend on high speed for 30 seconds, or until smooth.

In a large heavy-bottomed pot (preferably a Dutch oven) over medium-high heat, heat 1 Tbsp of the oil. Generously season the beef with salt and pepper. Working in batches, sear the beef on all sides, 6 to 8 minutes. Transfer the beef to a plate.

Lower the heat to medium. Add the remaining 1 Tbsp oil to the pot along with the onion and garlic. Cook for 5 minutes, or until the onion softens. If it starts to stick, add a splash of water and scrape up

any stuck bits. Add the cumin, oregano, and chili powder. Cook for 30 seconds, stirring frequently. Add the tomatoes and their juices, crushing the tomatoes as you add them to the pot. Return the beef and any accumulated juices to the pot. Stir in the poblano purée, and bring the mixture to a boil over high heat. Turn the heat to low and simmer, uncovered, for 1½ to 2 hours, until the liquid thickens and the beef is tender.

Stir in the beans and cook for about 10 minutes more. Serve with a fixin's bar of sour cream, corn chips or tortilla chips, chopped fresh cilantro, diced jalapeño chile, and diced avocado.

MAKE AHEAD

This dish can be made several days in advance and reheated over medium-low heat.

Grilled Flank Steak with Charred Poblano Romesco

Grilled flank steak was one of the first dishes I mastered—I think I served it at every single dinner party we hosted after we first got married. It really doesn't require marinating—a little salt, pepper, olive oil, and a really good sear are all it needs to shine. I love it with a buttery red wine sauce (page 179) or a bright herby chermoula (page 222), but this charred poblano romesco is my go-to sauce when it comes to really wowing guests. The steak is so simple to prepare, I like to spend some time on a really impressive sauce.

SERVES 4 TO 6

FOR THE FLANK STEAK

2 lb [910 g] beef flank steak

Kosher salt

Freshly ground black pepper

1 Tbsp olive oil

FOR THE CHARRED POBLANO ROMESCO

½ cup [120 ml] plus 1 Tbsp extra-virgin olive oil

2 poblano chiles

1 garlic clove, roughly chopped

½ serrano chile, seeded

½ cup [6 g] fresh cilantro leaves and stems

½ cup [70 g] roasted unsalted almonds

1 tsp kosher salt

2 scallions, roughly chopped

½ tsp smoked paprika

3 Tbsp fresh lime juice (from about 2 limes)

To make the flank steak: Remove the steak from the refrigerator 1 hour before grilling. Generously season with salt and pepper and rub the olive oil all over the meat.

To make the charred poblano romesco: Rub 1 Tbsp of the extra-virgin olive oil over the poblano peppers.

Preheat an outdoor grill to high heat for 15 minutes.

Place the steak and poblano chiles on the grill. Close the lid and cook for 6 to 8 minutes. Flip the steak and poblanos, re-close the lid, and cook for 3 to 5 minutes more. If you like your steak medium-rare,

cook it for the least amount of time, about 9 minutes total. Don't open the grill cover between flips; you want to keep it very hot in there! When your steak is done, check the poblanos. They should be charred all over. If they aren't, give them a few more minutes on the grill. Transfer the steak to a cutting board and allow to rest while you make the romesco sauce.

Let the poblanos cool slightly. Cut them in half and remove the seeds, stems, and about half the charred skin—not all of it! Place the poblano flesh in a food processor or blender and add the remaining

½ cup [120 ml] extra-virgin olive oil, along with the remaining romesco ingredients: 1 chopped garlic clove, ½ seeded serrano chile, ½ cup [6 g] fresh cilantro leaves and stems, ½ cup [70 g] roasted unsalted almonds, 1 tsp kosher salt, 2 roughly chopped scallions, and 3 Tbsp lime juice. Process until you have a slightly chunky purée. If needed, add 1 Tbsp of water at a time to reach the desired consistency.

Slice the steak as thinly as possible, diagonally against the grain (see Cooking School, page 114). Serve with the romesco and be impressed with your results!

MAKE AHEAD

To make the romesco sauce ahead of time, either pre-grill the poblanos before you grill the steak, or broil them according to the Beef Chili with All the Fixin's directions (see page 201).

TOOL TIP

No outdoor grill? Cook this steak according to the directions for the Open-Faced Flank Steak Sandwich with Blue Cheese Sauce (page 112).

DO YOUR THING

A traditional romesco sauce is made with roasted red peppers—use three to make this recipe. Eliminate the serrano and scallions. Use parsley instead of cilantro, and sherry vinegar instead of lime juice.

Harissa Braised Short Ribs

These short ribs are fall-off-the-bone, melt-in-your-mouth good. The harissa tomato braising sauce is slightly spicy, vinegary, and infused with a rich, meaty flavor. I love serving short ribs over polenta, but the meat and sauce are so good on their own that sometimes they're best simply served with good bread for sopping up all that sauce.

SERVES 4 TO 6

4 (about 3 lb [1.4 kg]) bone-in short ribs

Kosher salt

Freshly ground black pepper

1 Tbsp grapeseed oil

1 large yellow onion, diced

6 garlic cloves, minced

1 Tbsp harissa

1 Tbsp tomato paste

1 Tbsp all-purpose flour

One 28-oz [800-g] can whole peeled tomatoes and their juices

¾ cup [180 ml] red wine vinegar

Season the short ribs generously with salt and pepper. In a large Dutch oven over medium-high heat, warm the grapeseed oil. Working in two batches, sear all four sides on the short ribs for 1 to 2 minutes per side, or until a golden crust forms. Transfer the short ribs to a clean surface (I place them on the lid of the Dutch oven so I don't have to clean an extra plate!) and pour off all but 1 Tbsp fat from the pot.

Add the onion and garlic. Cook, stirring often, for 2 to 3 minutes, or until the onion is browned. Add the harissa, tomato paste, and flour. Stir for 30 seconds to combine. Add the tomatoes and vinegar and bring the mixture to a boil over high heat.

Turn the heat to low. Use tongs to nestle the short ribs, bone-side up, into the tomato sauce and pour in any juices that have collected. Cover the pot and simmer for about 2½ hours, until the meat pulls easily off the bone.

MAKE AHEAD

Short ribs are actually best made the day before, refrigerated, and reheated to serve. Don't scrape off the hardened fat that rises to the surface when refrigerated; it's an important part of the sauce and will melt back into it when you reheat everything.

MAKE IT A MEAL

Start by sharing a platter of Grilled Artichoke with Miso Lemon Butter (page 220). Serve the short ribs with a loaf of really good, crusty bread, and/or over Classic Mashed Potatoes (page 180), or cauliflower rice if you're counting calories.

Chipotle Carnitas Tacos

Pork shoulder is the cheapest, most reliable, and foolproof way to feed a crowd. You can typically find it for $2 per lb [455 g]—meaning you can feed a crowd of ten for roughly $15 including tortillas and toppings! Because we like to host big dinner parties on a newlywed dime, carnitas are on regular rotation. We serve tacos and nothing else—no rice and beans necessary; these carnitas are good enough to carry the meal on their own.

SERVES 8 TO 10

FOR THE CHIPOTLE CARNITAS

One (4- to 5-lb [1.8- to 2.3-kg]) boneless, skinless pork shoulder or pork butt (same thing!)

Kosher salt

Freshly ground black pepper

2 Tbsp grapeseed oil

3 Tbsp brown sugar

2 canned chipotle chiles in adobo sauce, seeded and minced

2 Tbsp adobo sauce (from the same can)

2 garlic cloves, grated

Zest of 1 lime

1 tsp dried oregano

1 white onion, finely chopped

2 bay leaves

Juice of 1 lime

1 cup [240 ml] beef broth

½ cup [120 ml] fresh orange juice (from about 2 oranges)

FOR THE TACO FIXINGS

24 corn and/or flour tortillas

1 white onion, finely chopped

2 or 3 avocados, cubed

Store-bought pico de gallo or tomato salsa for serving

1 bunch fresh cilantro leaves (only), roughly chopped

Cotija cheese for topping

Preheat the oven to 400°F [200°C].

To make the chipotle carnitas: Rinse the pork shoulder and pat dry with paper towels. Liberally season with salt and pepper. In a Dutch oven over medium-high heat, heat the grapeseed oil. Sear the pork shoulder for 3 to 4 minutes per side, until golden brown. Transfer the pork to a plate and remove the Dutch oven from the heat.

In a small bowl, stir together the brown sugar, minced chipotle chiles, adobo sauce, garlic, lime zest, and oregano. When cool enough to handle, rub the chipotle paste all over the pork. Return the pork to the Dutch oven, fat-side up, and place the onion and bay leaves around it. Pour the lime juice, beef broth, and orange juice around the pork (not over it).

continued

Put the pot in the oven. Roast the pork, uncovered, for 30 minutes. Lower the heat to 250°F [120°C], cover the pot, and roast the pork for 6 to 7 hours more.

Let the pork rest in its juices for at least 10 minutes. Use clean hands or tongs to pull the meat apart, saturating it in the juice.

To prepare the fixings: Wrap four stacks of 6 tortillas each in aluminum foil and warm in a 300°F [150°C] oven for 15 to 20 minutes. Set out the tortillas, the beef carnitas, chopped onion, avocado, pico de gallo (or salsa), chopped cilantro, and Cotija cheese for a DIY taco buffet!

MAKE AHEAD

This pork is so forgiving; being reheated won't hurt it. Cook the pork as directed, shred, cool, and refrigerate until you're ready to serve. Reheat, covered, at 300°F [150°C] for about 30 minutes until warmed through.

COOKING SCHOOL

Set it and forget it: Make your carnitas in a slow cooker. Cook for about 8 hours on low heat, or for about 6 hours on high heat, depending on the size of your pork shoulder. If you're really pressed for time, you can skip the searing step if you want, but it adds an extra layer of delicious flavor.

SPECIAL INGREDIENT

Transfer the remaining chipotle chile in adobo sauce to a small jar or airtight container and refrigerate. It will keep for up to 1 month. Try blending it into soups such as the Chipotle Butternut Squash Soup with Crunchy Croutons (page 104), stirring it into mayonnaise for sandwiches, serving it with Crispy Smashed Potatoes (page 52), or blending it with olive oil to toss onto vegetables and roast.

BUY SMART

If you don't have 7 hours to cook, ask your butcher to cut the pork roast into 2-in [5-cm] cubes and follow the directions here. The meat will cook much faster, finishing in about 3 hours versus 7 hours.

Sides

AND

Vegetables

This chapter is titled "Sides and Vegetables," but, in reality, each of these dishes can stand on its own. At our house, we like to eat vegetarian a couple of nights a week, so dinner is often a mixed bag of three or four different veggie sides. I love mixing and matching flavors and ethnic backgrounds—say, a plate piled high with Crispy Brussels Sprouts with Spicy Orange Sauce (page 228), Grilled Carrots with Chermoula and Lemon Yogurt (page 222), and Grilled Artichoke with Miso Lemon Butter (page 220). These sides also pair beautifully with the entrées from the three dinner chapters—look for "Make It a Meal" tips, but there is really no wrong combination!

Greek Potatoes

Red potatoes and fennel are roasted until soft and creamy on the inside and crispy on the outside, and are then tossed in an herby, vinegary sauce that they soak up while still hot. Then they're topped with olives, feta, and Pickled Red Onions (page 82).

SERVES 4 TO 6

2 lb [910 g] small red-skinned potatoes, quartered

1 large fennel bulb, trimmed and cut into ¼-in-by-1-in [6-mm-by-2.5-cm] slices

3 Tbsp extra-virgin olive oil

2 tsp kosher salt

⅛ tsp freshly ground black pepper

3 garlic cloves, minced

¼ cup [10 g] finely chopped fresh parsley, plus more for garnishing

¼ cup [10 g] finely chopped fresh dill

1 Tbsp champagne vinegar

½ cup [45 g] chopped pitted Kalamata olives

½ cup [60 g] crumbled feta cheese

¼ cup [40 g] Pickled Red Onions (page 82)

Preheat the oven to 425°F [220°C]. Line a large baking sheet, or two smaller sheets, with aluminum foil.

In a large bowl, toss together the potatoes, fennel, 2 Tbsp of the extra-virgin olive oil, the salt, and pepper until evenly coated. Transfer to the prepared baking sheet(s). Spread out the vegetables so they do not touch. Don't wash that bowl just yet; you'll use it again. Cook for 50 minutes, flipping halfway through the cooking time.

In that same large bowl, whisk the garlic, parsley, dill, remaining 1 Tbsp extra-virgin olive oil, and the vinegar.

Once cooked, transfer the hot potatoes and fennel to the bowl with the dressing and toss to coat.

Transfer the potatoes to a large serving dish and sprinkle with the olives, feta, and pickled red onions. Garnish with parsley and serve immediately.

LEFTOVER ARE A GOOD THING

Stir a bit of mayonnaise into any leftovers for a Greek potato salad.

MAKE IT A MEAL

These potatoes have so much going on that you can get away with using really simple accompaniments. Butter lettuce tossed in Apple Cider Vinaigrette (page 91) and grilled chicken thighs make perfect accompaniments. Or, toss some plain pulled chicken with the potatoes and fennel and call it a (delicious) meal.

Cherry Tomato and Fried Goat Cheese Salad

One summer, George and I spent a lot of time on Nantucket with our friends the Wick family, and our friend Lily and I often took it upon ourselves to cook the most lavish feasts we could dream up. We'd scheme our menus in the morning and set out on hours-long quests—to the stand near town for the best corn; to the farm near the beach for the greatest tomatoes on the East Coast; to the fishmonger for shrimp; and, finally, to Bartlett's for one of their famous blueberry pies. The best days are those when the only care in the world is to put the best dinner on the table for family and friends to gather around. This Cherry Tomato and Fried Goat Cheese Salad was born when we found the sweetest, ripest cherry tomatoes imaginable one July day. We knew we had to do something simple, but decadent, to compliment them—enter: fried goat cheese.

SERVES 4 TO 6

1 medium shallot, thinly sliced (or 3 Tbsp Pickled Red Onions, page 82, if you have them!)

½ cup [120 ml] red wine vinegar

¼ cup [60 ml] water

1 Tbsp sugar

½ tsp kosher salt

2 pints [600 g] mixed cherry tomatoes, halved

1 bunch fresh basil, cut into chiffonade (see Cooking School, page 40; about ¾ cup [15 g])

2 Tbsp extra-virgin olive oil

2 Tbsp fresh lemon juice (from about 1 lemon)

Pinch of freshly ground black pepper

4 or 5 pieces Fried Goat Cheese (facing page)

In a small saucepan over high heat, combine the shallot, vinegar, water, sugar, and ¼ teaspoon of the salt. Bring to a boil and lower the heat to medium. Cook for 4 to 5 minutes, stirring often, or until the shallot softens. Remove from the heat, set the pan aside, and let the shallots continue to steep in the vinegar mixture until ready for use, at least 10 minutes. Drain.

In a shallow serving bowl, combine the tomatoes with the basil, pickled shallots, extra-virgin olive oil, lemon juice, the remaining ¼ teaspoon salt, and the pepper. Gently toss to combine. Arrange the fried goat cheese over the top and serve immediately.

MAKE AHEAD

The fried goat cheese can be made several hours in advance and kept at room temperature until serving.

DO YOUR THING

If you're looking for a greens-based salad, toss in several handfuls of arugula at the last minute.

BACK POCKET RECIPE

Fried Goat Cheese

While these little coins of fried goat cheese are sensational over a hearty salad (like the Farmers' Market Salad with Apple Cider Vinaigrette, page 91, or a summer side like the Cherry Tomato and Fried Goat Cheese Salad, facing page), they're also fantastic on their own. Drizzle them with a bit of balsamic glaze or serve with a jarred tomato sauce and you're set.

SERVES 2 TO 4

One 4-oz [115-g] log goat cheese	1 large egg
⅓ sleeve of Saltine crackers	1 tsp water
½ cup [70 g] all-purpose flour	Grapeseed oil for frying

Freeze the goat cheese for 20 minutes to 1 hour before using.

In a food processor, blend the crackers to a powder and transfer to a shallow bowl. In a second shallow bowl, place the flour. In a third shallow bowl, whisk the egg with the water.

Slice the goat cheese into 4 or 5 thick slices. Coat the slices in this order: in flour first, in egg, and in crushed saltines.

In a medium skillet or saucepan over medium heat, heat ½ in [12 mm] grapeseed oil. When you think the oil is hot enough, throw in a cracker crumb. If it sizzles, it's ready. Cook the goat cheese for 2 to 3 minutes on each side, or until golden brown. Transfer to a paper towel-lined plate to absorb any excess oil.

DO YOUR THING

Use ½ cup [30 g] panko bread crumbs, crushed pretzels, or any other crushed cracker you like in place of the Saltines. Stir seasonings such as garlic powder or cayenne pepper into the flour, if desired.

Couscous with Beets and Arugula

This was one of my go-to dishes when I was catering. It's absolutely gorgeous (the beets turn the couscous hot pink!), and it pairs beautifully with so many foods. We love serving it at our annual friends' Easter brunch we've hosted every year since we got married for all the other California transplants with no family nearby.

SERVES 2

1 large (about 8-oz [230-g]) beet, root end removed, peeled with a vegetable peeler, and cut into ½-in [12-mm] cubes

1 Tbsp plus 2 tsp extra-virgin olive oil

½ tsp kosher salt

⅛ tsp freshly ground black pepper

½ cup [120 ml] water

Juice of 1 lemon

½ cup [90 g] dry instant couscous

1 tsp white balsamic vinegar

3 Tbsp finely chopped fresh parsley

½ cup [10 g] packed baby arugula

2 oz [55 g] crumbled feta cheese

2 Tbsp chopped roasted salted hazelnuts

Preheat the oven to 400°F [200°C].

Place the cut beets on a rimmed baking sheet and toss with 2 tsp of the olive oil, ¼ tsp of the salt, and the pepper. Roast for 35 to 40 minutes, until the beets are easily pierced with a fork.

Meanwhile, cook the couscous. In a small pot over high heat, bring the water to a boil. Remove the pot from the heat and stir in the lemon juice, the remaining ¼ tsp salt, and the couscous. Cover the pot and let sit for 10 minutes.

Fluff the couscous with a fork and transfer it to a medium bowl. Stir in the roasted beets, the remaining 1 Tbsp olive oil, the vinegar, and parsley. Gently toss in the arugula and feta. Transfer to a shallow serving bowl, sprinkle with the hazelnuts, and serve at room temperature.

DO YOUR THING

Try a different roasted chopped vegetable than the beets, like cauliflower, carrots, or fennel.

MAKE IT A MEAL

Make it an entrée salad: Triple the amount of arugula and top with cubed avocado and whatever cooked protein you have on hand. It's great with grilled shrimp.

BUY SMART

Most major grocery stores sell arugula in bulk bins. Buy just the ½ cup [10 g] needed for this recipe if you don't think you'll use an entire container. Most stores also sell precooked beets.

Beet and Potato Hash

In the diner breakfast decision-making battle ("fruit cup or hash browns?"), hash browns should *always* win. My beet and potato hash is a fresh, grown-up version (no offense—love you, diner hash browns) of the frozen hash browns that diners everywhere sling pounds of daily.

SERVES 4 TO 6

2 Tbsp grapeseed oil

1 large yellow onion, cut into ¼-in [6-mm] pieces

3 large garlic cloves, minced

2 large (about 1½ lb [680 g]) Yukon Gold potatoes, scrubbed clean and cut into ½-in [12-mm] cubes

1 lb [455 g] beets, peeled and cut into ½-in [12-mm] cubes

1 cup [240 ml] water

1 Tbsp fresh thyme leaves

1 tsp kosher salt

½ tsp garlic powder

¼ tsp smoked paprika

¼ tsp red pepper flakes

4 oz [115 g] feta cheese

2 Tbsp chopped fresh parsley

In a large nonstick skillet over medium heat, warm 1 Tbsp of the oil. Add the onion and cook for 3 minutes. Add the garlic, potatoes, beets, and water and stir to combine. Cook for 15 to 20 minutes, stirring occasionally.

Stir in the thyme, salt, garlic powder, paprika, and red pepper flakes. Cook for 20 to 25 minutes more, stirring occasionally, until the beets and potatoes are fork-tender. If the water evaporates and the hash is sticking to the pan before the vegetables are fork-tender, add ¼ cup [60 ml] more water at a time.

When the potatoes and beets are fork-tender and the water has evaporated, drizzle the remaining 1 Tbsp grapeseed oil over the top. Turn the heat to medium-high and sauté for several minutes to brown the hash. Transfer to a serving bowl, sprinkle the feta cheese and parsley over the top, and serve hot or at room temperature.

DO YOUR THING

I like to leave the skins on my potatoes, but go ahead and peel them if you prefer.

MAKE IT A MEAL

Though I originally served this recipe for a brunch spread, I find myself cooking it for dinner more than breakfast. It's great alongside Fig-Glazed Pork Belly (page 183), Spatchcocked Chicken with the Best Ever Green Sauce (page 176), or simply with a Poached Egg (page 48) on top. Adding a bit of sausage into the hash isn't a bad idea either.

COOKING SCHOOL

With a name like "hash," this dish ain't gonna be pretty. Know that the potatoes will stick to the pan, they'll fall apart, and your hash will generally look a little wonky. Don't fret—it'll be delicious!

Asparagus with Mustard Butter and Soft-Boiled Eggs

During the summer we spent in Telluride, Colorado, we met the loveliest couple who invited us for lunch at their farm and vineyard. When we arrived, they took us on a tour of the farm, handed us a pair of shears and a hand trowel, and, together, we harvested all the ingredients for our farm-straight-to-table lunch. One of the dishes we made was buttery green beans with hard-boiled eggs—so simple, but so memorable because of the freshness of the ingredients and the joy of cooking together in the kitchen with wine in hand. This dish is inspired by that afternoon at Sutcliffe Vineyards.

SERVES 2 TO 4

1 lb [455 g] asparagus, trimmed	¼ tsp kosher salt
2 Tbsp unsalted butter	⅛ tsp freshly ground black pepper
2 garlic cloves, minced	2 Soft-Boiled Eggs (page 48)
1 Tbsp sherry vinegar	Maldon sea salt
3 tsp coarse-grain mustard	1 Tbsp chopped fresh herbs

Fill a large skillet with 1 in [2.5 cm] salted water and bring it to a boil over high heat. Add the asparagus and cook for 2 to 4 minutes, depending on the size of the spears, until bright green and just fork-tender. Drain the asparagus and transfer to a paper towel-lined plate.

Wipe out the skillet, place it over medium heat, and add the butter to melt. Add the garlic and cook for about 30 seconds, until light golden. Whisk in the vinegar, mustard, kosher salt, and pepper. Add the asparagus and toss to coat. Transfer the asparagus to a platter and drizzle the mustard butter over the top. Cut the eggs in half, place alongside the asparagus, and garnish with sea salt and the herbs.

SEASONALITY

Depending on the season, swap green beans, white asparagus, or snap peas for the asparagus.

SPECIAL INGREDIENT

I love coarse-grain mustard, which is basically a hybrid of Dijon and whole-grain mustard. If you don't have it, use Dijon or whole-grain instead—no need to buy a new ingredient here, unless you really like mustard!

Grilled Artichoke with Miso Lemon Butter

A certain stretch of Highway 1, the idyllic highway that runs along California's coast, is littered with roadside farm stands hawking their goods for impossibly low prices. A single artichoke in a grocery store can run you $5, while they are selling ten for $1 in Castroville! Whether they're 10 cents or $5, there's no denying that artichokes are a novelty of a vegetable, and worth every penny. They can seem a bit intimidating to prepare, but this is my foolproof method for a tender, lightly charred artichoke and a dipping sauce you'll want to dip everything in sight into.

SERVES 2 AS A SIDE, 4 AS AN APPETIZER

FOR THE ARTICHOKE

1 large artichoke

2 tsp grapeseed oil

FOR THE MISO LEMON BUTTER

3 Tbsp unsalted butter

1 Tbsp miso paste

1 Tbsp fresh lemon juice (from about ½ lemon)

⅛ tsp freshly ground black pepper

To make the artichoke: Bring a large pot filled with several quarts of salted water to a boil over high heat.

Preheat a grill to medium-high heat.

Use a serrated knife to trim 1 to 2 in [2.5 to 5 cm] off the top of the artichoke, cutting all the pointed ends off the top leaves. Use kitchen shears to cut the points off the remaining leaves. Trim and pull off any small leaves from the stalk. Cut the artichoke in half through the stem.

Add the artichoke halves to the boiling water and cook for about 15 minutes, covered, until fork-tender. Drain, shaking any excess water out of the leaves. Holding the hot artichoke halves with a kitchen towel, use a spoon to scrape out the fuzzy choke and the purple prickly leaves surrounding it. You can also scrape the choke out before cooking, but it's a lot easier once it's cooked.

Rub the grapeseed oil on the cut side of the artichoke and place it, cut-side down, on the preheated grill, keeping the lid open. Cook for 3 minutes, flip, and cook for 1 to 2 minutes more on the leaf side until the tips of the leaves are slightly charred. Transfer to a plate.

To make the miso lemon butter: While the artichoke cooks, in a small pot or saucepan over medium heat, combine the butter, miso paste, lemon juice, and pepper. Whisk to combine. When combined, remove from the heat and pour into a small serving vessel.

Put the artichoke halves, miso lemon butter, and an empty bowl for discarded leaves on a serving platter (I like to use a wooden board) and serve immediately.

SPECIAL INGREDIENT

A little miso paste goes a long way! You'll love the salty, unique flavor boost it adds to soups and salad dressings. Try the Miso Ginger Dressing (page 81) and Creamy Miso Mushroom Soup (page 102) for inspiration on new ways to use miso.

DO YOUR THING

The miso lemon butter is delicious on everything. Try it drizzled over grilled shrimp and grilled vegetables.

COOKING SCHOOL

Cooking the artichokes with a lid on will cause them to lose their vibrant green color, but since we are char-grilling them, it's no big deal and will speed up your cook time. If you want to keep them bright green, boil uncovered for about 18 minutes. If you want to forego the grilling step completely, boil uncovered for 20 minutes, or until the stem is fork-tender.

Grilled Carrots with Chermoula and Lemon Yogurt

With a bit of parboiling prep, *most* veggies are delicious cooked on the grill. Try this parboil-before-grilling technique for parsnips, sweet potatoes, fingerling potatoes, and radishes.

SERVES 4

FOR THE GRILLED CARROTS

2 lb [910 g] medium carrots, peeled and halved lengthwise

1 Tbsp grapeseed oil

½ tsp kosher salt

FOR THE CHERMOULA

½ cup [6 g] fresh cilantro leaves

½ cup [6 g] fresh parsley leaves

3 Tbsp grapeseed oil

Zest and juice of 1 lemon

1 tsp ground cumin

¼ tsp smoked paprika

⅛ tsp kosher salt

Pinch of red pepper flakes

FOR THE LEMON YOGURT

¼ cup [60 g] plain yogurt

½ tsp lemon zest

Juice of 1 lemon

Pinch of kosher salt

Preheat a grill to medium-high heat (see Tool Tip).

To make the carrots: Bring a large pot of salted water to a boil over high heat. Add the carrots and boil for about 10 minutes, until tender but not completely soft. Drain and pat dry with a dish towel. Transfer the carrots to a large bowl and toss with the oil and salt.

Place the carrots on the grill and close the lid. Cook for 8 to 10 minutes, flipping halfway through the cooking time. The carrots will have dark grill marks and slightly charred tips when they are ready.

To make the chermoula: In the small bowl of a food processor or blender, combine the cilantro, parsley, oil, lemon zest and juice, cumin, paprika, salt, and red pepper flakes, and process until chunky but combined. Taste and season with more salt, if needed.

To make the lemon yogurt: In a small bowl, stir together the yogurt, lemon zest and juice, and salt.

Spoon some lemon yogurt onto the bottom of a serving platter and top with the carrots and chermoula. Serve immediately.

TOOL TIP

If you don't have a grill, you can achieve a similar effect by boiling and then roasting the carrots at 425°F [220°C] for 25 to 30 minutes, until dark brown and cooked through.

Corn

Corn, glorious corn. Some of my earliest childhood memories are of shucking corn with my cousins on hot summer nights at the beach. During corn season in North Carolina, farmers pull up on the side of the road and sell sweet white corn straight out of their truck beds for pennies. Now, when George and I head to Bald Head Island, North Carolina, for my family's annual beach week, we pull over to buy a box full of corn and peaches for the week.

This corn salad borrows the basic formula of elote (Mexican corn) but swaps in Middle Eastern ingredients for an Israeli spin. Tahini, lemon juice, feta cheese, and fresh parsley take the place of mayonnaise, lime juice, Cotija cheese, and fresh cilantro in this simple, flavor-packed dish.

The second corn dish is a little taste of the South—a corn pudding that will be *the simplest thing you will ever make*. With no added ingredients, the starch alone in the corn pulls it together into a spoonbread-esque pudding that could rival any Southern grandmother's recipe.

Grilled Corn and Tahini Salad

One insanely lucky month in 2017, George and I flew directly from a work trip in Israel to our friends' wedding in Sayulita, Mexico. Two back-to-back weeks of eating our favorite foods on the planet—hummus, shakshuka, and sabich chased by tacos, guacamole, and margaritas. This corn dish was born directly after that trip—a fusion of flavors from those two parts of the world.

SERVES 4

5 ears fresh corn, shucked	3 oz [85 g] feta cheese, crumbled
1 Tbsp olive oil	4 Tbsp [10 g] finely chopped fresh parsley
2 Tbsp mayonnaise	½ tsp salt
1 Tbsp tahini	½ tsp chili powder
Juice of 1 lemon	Pinch of cayenne pepper

Preheat a grill to high heat (see Tool Tip).

Rub the shucked corn with the olive oil, place it on the grill, and close the cover. Cook for 2 to 3 minutes per side, until lightly charred all over.

In a large bowl, whisk the mayonnaise, tahini, lemon juice, 2 oz [55 g] of the feta cheese, 3 Tbsp of the parsley, the salt, chili powder, and cayenne pepper. When the corn is cool enough to handle, cut the kernels off the cob and add them to the bowl. Stir to combine. Transfer to a serving platter and sprinkle the remaining 1 oz [30 g] feta and 1 Tbsp parsley over the top.

TOOL TIP

If you don't own a grill, cook the corn under the broiler for 9 to 10 minutes, rotating each side once it is charred, after about 3 minutes.

COOKING SCHOOL

The easiest way to cut corn off the cob is to stand the cob on its stem end, and cut down the side, rotating the cob to cut all sides.

BUY SMART

Don't buy fresh corn if it isn't corn season where you live (ask your grocer). Buy frozen and use ¾ cup [105 g] kernels per ear of corn (3 cups total [315 g]) for this recipe.

Corn "Pudding"

This is hands down the easiest recipe in this entire book. It is also one of the most decadent, comforting dishes. Creamy, five-ingredient-only corn pudding awaits you.

SERVES 4

8 ears fresh sweet white corn, shucked

¼ tsp garlic powder

¼ tsp kosher salt

½ lime

1 Tbsp unsalted butter, quartered

Preheat the oven to 350°F [180°C]. Coat an 8-in [20-cm] nonstick ovensafe skillet with nonstick cooking spray.

Using the largest holes on a box grater, grate the corn down to the cob directly into the skillet. Use a spatula to smooth the corn evenly. Sprinkle the garlic powder and salt over the top. Put the skillet in the oven and bake for 20 to 25 minutes, or until light golden and firm to the touch.

Squeeze the fresh lime juice over and scatter the butter cubes on top (they'll melt into the pudding). Serve immediately.

SEASONALITY

Unfortunately, it's not worth trying to make this with frozen corn. Wait until sweet corn season (typically June through August) and make the most of it!

Crispy Brussels Sprouts with Spicy Orange Sauce

It was our accidental tradition that the night before George deployed, we would go out way too late, and eat and drink way too much. The hangover really cut the sadness the next day! The inspiration for this recipe comes from Leroy's in Coronado, California—the restaurant where we wiled away the hours before George's final SEAL deployment.

SERVES 2 TO 4

1 lb [455 g] Brussels sprouts, trimmed	1 Tbsp soy sauce
1½ Tbsp olive oil	1 Tbsp rice vinegar
½ tsp kosher salt	1½ tsp fish sauce
Juice of 3 large oranges	2 scallions, light green and white parts only, thinly sliced
1 Tbsp sambal oelek	

Preheat the oven to 450°F [230°C].

Halve small Brussels sprouts and quarter larger sprouts so all pieces are roughly the same size. Place the sprouts in a large bowl and toss with the olive oil and salt. Transfer to a baking sheet and spread out so no Brussels sprouts are touching. Place the baking sheet in the middle of the oven and roast for 25 to 30 minutes, stirring every 10 minutes or so, until the sprouts are dark brown and crispy.

While the Brussels sprouts cook, make the spicy orange sauce. In a small pot over high heat, combine the orange juice, sambal oelek, soy sauce, rice vinegar, and fish sauce. Bring to a boil. Lower the heat to medium and cook for 10 to 15 minutes, or until reduced to about 3 Tbsp. Keep a close watch; if you reduce it too far it will quickly burn.

Transfer the Brussels sprouts, spicy orange sauce, and scallions to a large bowl and toss to combine. Serve immediately.

DO YOUR THING

This sauce is delicious over just about any roasted veggie. Try it with cauliflower, broccoli, cabbage, edamame beans, beets, or carrots.

COOKING SCHOOL

Cooking the sprouts directly on the baking sheet (rather than lining it with aluminum foil) leads to crispier sprouts. However, it will also lead to a tougher cleanup, so choose your battles!

BUY SMART

If you already have Sriracha, use it in place of sambal oelek in the same quantity.

Baby Bok Choy and Brown Rice Stir-Fry

Stir-fries are our go-to "odds-and-ends" meal. We almost always have brown rice lurking in the fridge or pantry, and always have a fresh veggie on the brink of going bad. A little chopping, a great sauce, a big skillet, and a few minutes later you have an addictive main or side dish sitting before you. We really love the combo of brown rice and bok choy, but you can really use any vegetable; just adjust the cooking time as needed.

SERVES 2 AS A MEAL, 4 AS A SIDE

¾ cup [175 g] dry brown rice

3 Tbsp rice vinegar

2 Tbsp soy sauce

1 tsp sambal oelek

1 tsp honey

1 tsp toasted sesame oil

1 Tbsp grapeseed oil

½ small yellow onion, thinly sliced

3 garlic cloves, thinly sliced

3 baby bok choy, leafy tops removed and reserved, stalks cut into ¼-in- [6-mm-] thick ribbons

¼ cup [60 ml] water

Cook the brown rice (see the Quick Cooking Reference Guide on page 263).

In a small bowl, whisk the vinegar, soy sauce, sambal oelek, honey, and sesame oil.

In a large nonstick skillet over medium heat, warm the grapeseed oil. Add the onion and garlic, and cook for 4 to 5 minutes, stirring frequently, or until the onion softens. Add the bok choy stalks and water. Cook for 2 to 3 minutes, stirring frequently, until all the water evaporates. Add the stir-fry sauce, brown rice, and bok choy greens. Cook for 2 to 3 minutes more, until the greens wilt. Serve hot or at room temperature.

SEASONALITY

Swap in kale, spinach, Swiss chard, broccolini, or even asparagus for the bok choy. Cook until wilted or tender, depending on the veggie.

MAKE IT A MEAL

Top with a Soft-Fried Egg (page 47) or Poached Egg (page 48), or serve alongside Honey & Garlic Salmon (page 146).

Roasted Cabbage with Brown Butter Bread Crumbs

I can't tell you how many people have exclaimed, "I had no idea I liked cabbage!" after trying this dish. This is one of the cheapest, tastiest dishes in my repertoire, and it creates lifetime cabbage converts.

SERVES 2 TO 4

1 head green cabbage, cut into 2-in- [5-cm-] thick wedges

2 Tbsp olive oil

Juice and zest of 1 lemon

1¼ tsp kosher salt

2 Tbsp unsalted butter

½ cup [30 g] panko bread crumbs

¼ cup [10 g] finely chopped fresh parsley

3 Tbsp balsamic glaze

Preheat the oven to 400°F [200°C]. Line a baking sheet with parchment paper.

Lay the cabbage wedges flat on the prepared baking sheet so they do not overlap. Drizzle with the olive oil and lemon juice. Season with 1 tsp of the salt. Roast for 45 to 50 minutes, until tender and browned on the outside leaves.

Meanwhile, in a medium nonstick skillet over medium-low heat, melt the butter. Gently swirl it occasionally and cook for 4 to 6 minutes, until the butter turns light brown. Add the bread crumbs, remaining ¼ tsp salt, and the lemon zest, toss, and cook for about 3 minutes, until the bread crumbs are golden brown. Cool. Stir in the parsley.

Use a spatula to carefully transfer the cabbage (it will fall apart if you aren't careful!) to a large serving platter. Drizzle with the balsamic glaze and scatter the bread crumbs over the top. Serve immediately.

DO YOUR THING

Make this a more indulgent dish by crumbling goat cheese or feta cheese over top. Or, forego the balsamic glaze and bread crumbs and drizzle the cabbage with rice vinegar, soy sauce, Sriracha, and sesame seeds for some Asian flare.

MAKE IT A MEAL

Serve alongside the Fig-Glazed Pork Belly (page 183). The acidity in the cabbage dish cuts nicely through the sweet fattiness of the fig-glazed pork.

BUY SMART

Cabbage head sizes can vary widely. Buy a small head if you're cooking for two, or a really large one if you're cooking for four to six. Or, halve the recipe and use the other cabbage half as salad greens for the Crunchy-Tangy Vietnamese Chicken Salad (page 83).

Charred Broccoli with Sriracha Almond Butter Sauce

Roasting broccoli until charred and crispy before dousing it in a spicy almond butter sauce is one sure way to convert any veggie hater into a lifelong broccoli advocate. If you're looking for a simple side, the broccoli cooked in soy sauce and lime juice is also wonderful on its own.

SERVES 4

1 lb [455 g] broccoli	2 Tbsp untoasted slivered almonds
1 Tbsp plus 1 tsp grapeseed oil	¼ cup [60 ml] Sriracha Almond Butter Sauce (page 234)
1 Tbsp soy sauce	
Juice of 1 lime	4 scallions, white and green parts, thinly sliced
½ cup [75 g] shelled edamame	

Use a vegetable peeler to peel the broccoli stems to remove their tough, chewy outer layer. Trim the tough ends and slice the stems ¼ in [6 mm] thick all the way up to the florets. Cut off the stems and put aside. Cut the florets into pieces no larger than 1 in [2.5 cm]. The size is important here, since you'll have undercooked broccoli if the pieces are too large.

In your largest nonstick skillet over medium-high heat, warm 1 Tbsp of the grapeseed oil. Add the broccoli stems (not florets) and cook for 4 minutes, stirring occasionally. Add the additional 1 tsp grapeseed oil, the broccoli florets, soy sauce, and lime juice and cook, stirring occasionally, for 5 minutes more. If the pan gets too dry, add 1 Tbsp water at a time. Lower the heat to medium. Add the edamame and almonds and cook for about 3 minutes more, until the nuts and edamame are lightly charred. Transfer the broccoli mixture to a serving platter, drizzle with the Sriracha almond butter sauce, and scatter the scallions over the top. Enjoy immediately or at room temperature.

SPECIAL INGREDIENT

Every time I buy untoasted slivered almonds, they seem to sit in the back of my cupboard collecting dust. Try throwing them into a granola, like the Hazelnut-Maple Granola (page 27), or making cashew milk (page 51).

MAKE IT A MEAL

Toss everything in a bowl with 8 oz [230 g] cooked soba noodles and a bit more sauce for a pad Thai–esque noodle dish.

Sriracha Almond Butter Sauce

A classic Thai peanut sauce is always welcomed. Here I sub almond butter for peanut butter for a richer, earthier flavor, not to mention the health upsides, like nearly three times the vitamin E and twice the iron.

MAKES ABOUT ¾ CUP [180 ML] SAUCE

½ cup [130 g] smooth almond butter

2 Tbsp toasted sesame oil

2 Tbsp soy sauce

3 Tbsp fresh lime juice
(from about 2 limes)

1 Tbsp plus 1 tsp Sriracha

1 tsp honey or maple syrup

2 garlic cloves, grated

In a medium bowl, stir together all the ingredients. Stir in 1 tsp warm water at a time until you've achieved a drizzle-able consistency.

LEFTOVERS ARE A GOOD THING

This batch makes triple the amount you need for the Charred Broccoli recipe (page 232). Drizzle leftover sauce on grilled chicken or shrimp, roasted cauliflower, or soba or zucchini zoodles.

DO YOUR THING

Swap peanut for almond butter for a more classic peanut sauce. Add diced jalapeño or Thai chiles for an even spicier sauce.

Desserts

When I hear people say, "I'm not really a dessert person," I instantly think to myself, *"You must be eating the wrong desserts."* Desserts can run such a gamut of textures and flavors, from cinnamon-y, chewy Churro Rice Krispies Treats (facing page), to spiced, juicy, tender Chai-Poached Honeycrisp Apples (page 250), to tart and creamy Lime Pie (page 255). There's something for everyone here! I love dessert not only for how tasty it is, but for how it drags out meals and dinner parties, begging them not to end. A shared dessert on a date night in is such a sweet way to cap off a romantic evening at home.

Churro Rice Krispies Treats

This dessert is a grown-up take on the nostalgic treat from our youth. It's so much fun to pull out a "nongourmet" dessert like this at the end of a fancy dinner party. The best part? They're so easy to make that I can task George with making them the night before, meaning we can stay out of the kitchen and be with our guests when it's time to serve dessert. This makes a small batch, perfect for a date night at home, so double or triple it for a crowd.

SERVES 4

2 Tbsp unsalted butter

5 oz [140 g] mini marshmallows (about half of a standard bag)

¼ tsp vanilla extract

2¼ cups [59.5 g] Rice Krispies cereal

2 tsp sugar

½ tsp ground cinnamon

¼ tsp Maldon sea salt

Line a 4-by-8-in [10-by-20-cm] loaf pan with parchment paper that's a big enough piece to hang over both sides of the pan.

In a large pot over medium-low heat, melt the butter. Stir in the marshmallows and, when almost completely melted, turn off the heat. Add the vanilla and continue stirring until smooth. Stir in the cereal 1 cup [26.5 g] at a time until fully incorporated. Use a spatula to transfer the marshmallow mixture to the prepared loaf pan and smooth the top.

In a small bowl, stir together the sugar, cinnamon, and salt. Sprinkle the sugar mixture over the marshmallow mixture and let set for at least 30 minutes.

Use the edges of the parchment to pull the treats out of the loaf pan, slice, and devour immediately. Tightly wrap any leftovers in plastic wrap, store at room temperature, and consume within 2 to 3 days.

SPECIAL INGREDIENT

Use leftover cereal to make Coronado Cookies (page 240).

DO YOUR THING

Try finely ground espresso powder and cocoa powder in place of cinnamon for a mocha treat.

Coronado Cookies

George and I were lucky to be "adopted" by the nicest family in Coronado, California, when he was stationed there with the Navy. Nancy makes these cookies in huge batches and freezes them so they're always ready when someone stops by. I've adapted the recipe slightly, because the original recipe is a heavily guarded family treasure.

MAKES ABOUT TWENTY 2-IN [5-CM] COOKIES

½ cup [1 stick (110 g)] unsalted butter, at room temperature, cut into small chunks

½ cup [130 g] smooth almond butter

½ cup [100 g] granulated sugar

½ cup [100 g] firmly packed light brown sugar

1 large egg

1 tsp vanilla extract

1 cup [140 g] all-purpose flour

½ tsp baking soda

½ tsp salt

1 cup [180 g] semisweet chocolate baking chunks

1 cup [26.5 g] Rice Krispies cereal

½ cup [50 g] old-fashioned rolled oats

½ cup [70 g] golden raisins (optional)

Preheat the oven to 375°F [190°C]. Line two baking sheets with parchment paper.

In the bowl of a stand mixer fixed with the paddle attachment, or in a large bowl with a handheld mixer on medium-high speed, cream the butter, almond butter, granulated sugar and brown sugar together until fluffy and smooth, about 4 to 6 minutes. Scrape down the sides of the bowl, as needed. Add the egg and vanilla and continue beating until smooth.

In a small bowl, whisk the flour, baking soda, and salt until combined and no lumps remain.

Reduce the mixer speed to low and gradually incorporate the flour mixture into the butter mixture. Once fully incorporated, fold in the chocolate, Rice Krispies, oats, and raisins (if using). Turn the mixer off immediately once all ingredients are mixed in (over-mixing your dough will make the cookies tough).

Use a 1-Tbsp scoop to drop the dough 2 in [5 cm] apart on the prepared baking sheet. Bake for 8 to 10 minutes, or until the edges have lightly browned but the tops are still very blond. Let the cookies cool slightly, then transfer to a wire rack to cool completely.

MAKE AHEAD

Freeze cookie dough so freshly baked cookies are always just minutes away. Line a baking sheet with parchment paper, drop Tbsp-size dough balls on it (they can be close together!), freeze for 2 hours, and transfer the frozen dough balls to an airtight container to keep frozen. Bake frozen at 375°F [190°C] for 11 to 14 minutes.

DO YOUR THING

Swap peanut putter for almond butter and dried cranberries or dried cherries for the raisins.

North Carolina Wedding Cookies

George's grandmother, Deepe, was famous for these light, crumbly, delicious little cookies. When I asked my mother-in-law for the recipe, I realized they're really just Italian wedding cookies with a Southern spin—pecans instead of almonds. They make a perfect housewarming or Christmas present in a pretty little bag with a big bow and are a perfect wedding or shower treat.

MAKES ABOUT 30 SMALL COOKIES

¾ cup [1½ sticks (165 g)] unsalted butter, at room temperature

½ cup [60 g] powdered sugar

1 Tbsp vanilla extract

⅛ tsp kosher salt

2 cups [280 g] all-purpose flour, sifted

1 cup [120 g] finely ground pecans

Preheat the oven to 350°F [180°C]. Line a baking sheet with parchment paper.

In the bowl of a stand mixer fixed with the paddle attachment, or in a large bowl with a handheld mixer, on medium-high speed, beat the butter, ¼ cup [30 g] of the powdered sugar, the vanilla, and salt until pale and fully combined, 3 to 5 minutes.

Turn the mixer to low speed and slowly incorporate the flour and pecans, waiting until each addition is fully incorporated before adding the next. Cover and chill the dough for 2 hours.

Roll the dough into 1-in [2.5-cm] balls and place them 1 in [2.5 cm] apart on the prepared baking sheet. Bake for 15 to 20 minutes. They should not brown at all. Transfer to a wire rack to cool slightly.

Put the remaining ¼ cup [30 g] powdered sugar into a shallow bowl. While the cookies are still warm, roll them in the sugar. Return to the wire rack to continue cooling.

MAKE AHEAD

When sealed in an airtight container, these cookies will stay delicious for up to 5 days.

DO YOUR THING

Swap in almonds, walnuts, hazelnuts, or pistachios for the pecans in this recipe.

Pound Cake

These recipes come from my mother-in-law, Marsha, and will soon become part of your rotation.

Banana-Almond Pound Cake

MAKES 1 TUBE CAKE OR TWO 8-INCH LOAF CAKES

1 lb (4 sticks [455 g]) unsalted butter, at room temperature

1 lb [455 g] granulated sugar

5 large eggs, at room temperature

1 lb [455 g] all-purpose flour

1 tsp baking powder

¼ tsp kosher salt

5 bananas

1 Tbsp sour cream

2 tsp almond extract

1 tsp vanilla extract

¼ cup [30 g] powdered sugar

1 cup [120 g] fresh berries (whatever is in season)

Whipped cream or jam for topping (optional)

Preheat the oven to 325°F [165°C]. Coat a 10-in [25-cm] tube cake pan with nonstick cooking spray.

In the bowl of a stand mixer with the paddle attachment, or in a large bowl with a handheld mixer, on high speed, cream the butter and granulated sugar, beating for about 4 minutes until light and fluffy. Scrape down the sides of the bowl, as needed. With the mixer on low speed, add the eggs one at a time, fully incorporating each before adding the next.

In another large bowl, whisk the flour, baking powder, and salt.

In a medium bowl, mash the bananas. Stir in the sour cream, almond extract, and vanilla.

With the mixer on low speed, alternate adding the flour mixture and the banana mixture one-third at a time. Let each addition incorporate fully. Turn off the mixer immediately once the last addition is incorporated. *It's very important not to overmix the cake batter or you'll have a dense, tough cake.*

Pour the batter into the prepared pan and bake for about 1 hour and 15 minutes, or until a toothpick inserted in the middle of the cake comes out clean. Rotate the pan once, halfway through the cooking time. Cool the cake in the pan on a wire rack for 20 minutes. Carefully turn it out onto the wire rack by placing the wire rack over the pan and gently flipping both rack and pan over, tapping gently on top of the pan while pulling it up to allow the cake to slide out. When the cake is completely cool, transfer to a cake plate. Use a sifter or fine-mesh sieve to sprinkle the powdered sugar over the top. Add fresh berries or topping, if desired.

Meyer Lemon and Blueberry Pound Cake

MAKES 1 TUBE CAKE OR TWO 8-INCH LOAF CAKES

1 cup (2 sticks, [220 g]) butter, at room temperature, plus more for the pan

3½ cups [700 g] granulated sugar

6 eggs, at room temperature, separated

Zest of 2 Meyer lemons

1 tsp vanilla extract

3 cups [490 g] plus 2 Tbsp all-purpose flour

¼ teaspoon baking soda

1 cup (8 oz) sour cream

1½ cups [210 g] fresh blueberries, plus more for serving

½ cup [120 ml] plus 4 Tbsp Meyer lemon juice

2 cups [240 g] powdered sugar

Preheat the oven to 325°F [165°C]. Butter and flour a 10-in [25-cm] tube pan, or two 8-in [20-cm] loaf pans.

In the bowl of a stand mixer with the paddle attachment, or in a large bowl with a handheld mixer, on high speed, cream the butter and 3 cups [600 g] of the sugar, beating for about 4 minutes until light and fluffy. Scrape down the sides of the bowl, as needed. With the mixer on low speed, add the egg yolks one at a time, fully incorporating each before adding the next. Add the zest of 1 lemon and the vanilla.

In a medium bowl, whisk together the 3 cups [420 g] of the flour and the baking soda.

With the mixer on low, alternate adding the flour mixture and sour cream, one-third at a time. Let each addition incorporate fully before adding the next. Turn off the mixer immediately once the last addition is incorporated.

In a separate bowl, and using clean beaters, beat the egg whites on medium-high until they hold stiff peaks, about 3 to 4 minutes. Toss the blueberries with the remaining 2 Tbsp flour.

Gently, using a spatula, fold the blueberries and egg whites into the cake batter.

Pour the batter into the prepared pan, and bake for about 1 hour, until a toothpick inserted into the middle of the cake comes out clean. Rotate the pan once, halfway through the cooking time.

Meanwhile, combine the remaining ½ cup [100 g] sugar and the ½ cup [120 ml] lemon juice in a small saucepan and cook over medium heat until the sugar has dissolved. Set the lemon syrup aside to cool.

Cool the cake in the pan on a wire rack for 10 minutes. Place the wire rack upside-down over the pan and gently flip both rack and pan over, tapping gently on top of the pan while pulling it up to allow the cake to slide out. Allow to completely cool, about 1 hour. Poke several tiny holes into the top of the cake and pour the lemon syrup over top.

To make a glaze, in a small bowl, whisk the powdered sugar with the remaining lemon zest and 3 Tbsp of the remaining lemon juice to start. Add the final 1 Tbsp lemon juice, if needed.

Pour the glaze on top and serve with blueberries.

Strawberry Shortcake with Basil Whipped Cream

My birthday is June 21, which meant, when I was growing up, my birthdays were pool parties and, instead of birthday cake, I requested strawberry shortcake. My mom is a wonderful cook, but a self-admitted disastrous baker, so my birthday shortcake usually had chunks removed from where she'd scraped off the burnt bits or it had stuck to the pan. She'd cover up all the imperfections with more whipped cream and strawberries than my 4-year-old friends and I knew what to do with. It was perfect. This recipe is a foolproof, amped-up version of that childhood birthday cake. Celebrating your grown-up birthday with another couple? Cut the shortcake dough into 4 squares instead of 2, and double the amount of strawberries.

SERVES 2

FOR THE MACERATED STRAWBERRIES

8 oz [230 g] fresh strawberries, hulled and diced

1 tsp granulated sugar

1 tsp fresh lemon juice

FOR THE SHORTCAKE

⅓ cup [45 g] all-purpose flour, plus more for dusting

3 Tbsp fine cornmeal

2⅛ tsp granulated sugar

½ tsp baking powder

⅛ tsp kosher salt

2 Tbsp cold unsalted butter

¼ cup [60 ml] heavy cream, plus more for brushing the cakes

FOR THE BASIL WHIPPED CREAM

¼ cup [3 g] fresh basil leaves

½ cup [120 ml] heavy cream

2 tsp powdered sugar

¼ tsp vanilla extract

Preheat the oven to 350°F [180°C]. Line a baking sheet with parchment paper.

To macerate the strawberries: In a medium bowl, stir together the strawberries, granulated sugar, and lemon juice. Set aside to macerate.

To make the shortcake: In a large bowl, stir together the flour, cornmeal, 2 tsp of the granulated sugar, the baking powder, and salt. Using the largest holes on a box grater, grate the butter into the flour and use your fingers to quickly pinch the flour mixture and butter together until only pea-size pieces remain. Stir in the heavy cream until a rough dough forms.

Dump the dough onto a floured work surface and use your hands to knead the dough together. Gently pat the dough into a $\frac{1}{2}$-in- [12-mm-] thick rectangle and cut in half to form two squares. Move the shortcakes to the prepared baking sheet, brush with the 2 Tbsp heavy cream, and sprinkle with the remaining $\frac{1}{8}$ tsp granulated sugar.

Bake for 20 to 25 minutes until golden brown. The shortcakes will look ready on the outside before they're cooked through on the inside—be sure to bake for at least 20 minutes! Set aside to cool.

To make the basil whipped cream: Tear the basil leaves and place them in a small saucepan with the heavy cream. Bring to a gentle simmer over medium-low heat. Remove from the heat, cover, and let steep for 25 minutes. Use a slotted spoon or pour the cream through a fine-mesh strainer to remove the basil. Refrigerate for at least 1 hour; the cream needs to be very cold to whip properly.

In the bowl of a stand mixer with the whisk attachment, or in a large bowl with a handheld mixer, combine the basil cream, powdered sugar, and vanilla. Start whipping on low speed until the cream thickens slightly. Turn to high speed and whip until the cream holds stiff peaks, 1 to 2 minutes.

To serve, cut each shortbread in half horizontally, spoon whipped cream and strawberries over the bottom, and gently place the top over the strawberries. Serve immediately.

DO YOUR THING

Swap any summer fruit for strawberries. Peach short-cake is particularly lovely.

BUY SMART

Short on time? Buy an angel food cake at the store, and, as my mother would say, "gussy it up" with the macerated strawberries and basil whipped cream.

Chai-Poached Honeycrisp Apples

It's fun to end a meal with a really fancy, restaurant-quality dessert. Any sort of poached dessert certainly falls into that category, especially when dressed up with a chai syrup and the best vanilla ice cream you can find. Poaching fruit couldn't be easier, but it will make you look like a total pro.

SERVES 2

One 2-in [5-cm] piece fresh peeled ginger, sliced into thin strips

1 cup [200 g] sugar

1 Tbsp vanilla extract

1 tsp ground cinnamon

2 Honeycrisp apples or Pink Lady apples, halved and cored

2 chai teabags

½ pt [240 ml] vanilla ice cream

In a medium saucepan, combine the ginger, sugar, vanilla, cinnamon, and apples with enough water to cover the apples, about 4 to 6 cups [960 ml to 1.4 L]. Add the teabags and bring to a boil. Turn the heat to medium-low and cook the apples for 30 minutes, or until easily pierced with a fork.

Transfer the apples to a plate and discard the ginger and teabags. Return the pan to medium-high heat and continue cooking the poaching liquid for 6 to 7 minutes more, until reduced to a light syrup. You aren't making a caramel here; it should be syrupy, not thick.

Turn the heat to low and return the apples to the pan until ready to serve. Serve the apples with vanilla ice cream and a drizzle of chai syrup.

LEFTOVERS ARE A GOOD THING

If you're lucky enough to have leftover apples, chop them and serve with yogurt and granola for breakfast tomorrow morning!

MAKE AHEAD

Poach your apples up to 24 hours in advance. Refrigerate them in the pan with the syrup, and gently reheat over medium-low heat when ready to serve.

SEASONALITY

Try this recipe with whatever apple looks best at the market. Pears are also lovely when poached. Just reduce the cooking time to about 20 minutes.

Berry Crumble

This berry crumble's simplicity really allows the fruit's natural flavors to come through, so use the best, freshest fruit you can find. Put the crumble in the oven just before you sit down to eat and it'll be perfectly crisp and oozy by the end of a leisurely meal.

SERVES 2 TO 4

FOR THE OAT TOPPING

½ cup [50 g] old-fashioned rolled oats

½ cup [70 g] whole-wheat flour

6 Tbsp [85 g] unsalted butter, cubed, at room temperature

¼ cup [45 g] packed brown sugar

½ tsp vanilla extract

¼ tsp kosher salt

FOR THE BERRY FILLING

3 cups [560 g] mixed fresh berries, such as blueberries, blackberries, raspberries, and strawberries

Zest of ½ lemon

2 Tbsp fresh lemon juice (from about 1 lemon)

2 Tbsp granulated sugar

1 Tbsp cornstarch

¼ tsp kosher salt

Preheat the oven to 350°F [180°C].

To make the crumble: In a medium bowl, combine the oats, flour, butter, brown sugar, vanilla, and salt. Pinch the ingredients together with your fingers until combined into a rough dough. Refrigerate until needed.

To make the berry filling: If using strawberries, quarter them. In a large bowl, toss together the berries, lemon zest, lemon juice, granulated sugar, cornstarch, and salt. Pour the filling into an 8-in [20-cm] nonstick skillet or other similar size ovenproof dish.

Use your fingers to crumble the oat mixture into little pieces and scatter them over the berries. Place the skillet on a baking sheet and bake the crumble for 45 minutes to 1 hour, until the topping is golden brown and the filling bubbles up around the sides.

LEFTOVERS ARE A GOOD THING

My friend Lexie helped me fine-tune this recipe, so after cooking several variations at her place one day, I left her with a lot of leftover crumble. She ate it for breakfast all week with a scoop of Greek yogurt as parfait—genius!

SPECIAL INGREDIENT

While you can certainly use all-purpose flour in place of the whole-wheat flour here, the whole wheat adds a balancing earthy element to the bright sweetness of the fruit. It's worth keeping whole-wheat flour in your pantry and swapping in 1 to 2 Tbsp for all-purpose flour in recipes to add a nutty complexity to any baked good.

DO YOUR THING

Swap in any kind of stone fruit (peaches, plums, nectarines), for all or some of the berries. I love combining nectarines with blueberries and peaches with raspberries.

Rustic Cherry Pistachio Galette

Galettes are the lazy (or beginning) cook's solution to looking like a baking badass. Calling it "rustic" basically means you don't even have to provide an excuse if it comes out looking a little rough around the edges. In fact, the rougher the better! Feel free to swap in your favorite nut and whatever seasonal fruit looks best.

SERVES 4 TO 6

FOR THE CRUST

1 cup [140 g] all-purpose flour, plus more for dusting

1 tsp granulated sugar

⅛ tsp kosher salt

6 Tbsp [85 g] unsalted butter, cubed

1 Tbsp vodka

2 Tbsp water

1 large egg

1 Tbsp turbinado sugar (granulated sugar works, too)

FOR THE PISTACHIO FRANGIPANE

7 Tbsp [50 g] pistachios

¼ cup [50 g] granulated sugar

4 Tbsp [55 g] unsalted butter, at room temperature, cubed

1 large egg

1 Tbsp honey

2 tsp orange liqueur (brandy or bourbon work, too)

2 tsp orange zest

FOR THE CHERRY FILLING

12 oz [340 g] cherries, pitted and halved

1 Tbsp granulated sugar

2 tsp cornstarch

Powdered sugar for serving

To make the crust: In a large bowl, whisk the 1 cup flour, granulated sugar, and salt. Toss in the butter cubes and use your fingers to quickly pinch the butter and flour together until only pea-size crumbs remain. Stir in the vodka. Slowly pour in only as much water as needed to knead the mixture into a cohesive dough. Flatten the dough into a disk, cover, and refrigerate for at least 30 minutes.

To make the pistachio frangipane: In a blender or food processor, combine 6 Tbsp [43 g] of the pistachios, the granulated sugar, butter, egg, honey, liqueur, and orange zest and process on high speed until smooth.

To make the cherry filling: In a large bowl, toss the cherries, granulated sugar, and cornstarch together until the cornstarch dissolves.

continued

Preheat the oven to 375°F [190°C]. Line a baking sheet with parchment paper.

Assemble the galette: Flour the work surface liberally and use a rolling pin (or a wine bottle in a pinch!) to roll the dough into a 12-in [30.5-cm] circle, about ⅛ in [4 mm] thick. Carefully transfer the dough to the prepared baking sheet.

Leaving a 2-in [5-cm] border around the edges, spread the pistachio frangipane over the dough. Gently spoon the cherries over the top, discarding any accumulated juices. Fold the dough edges up over the filling. Since the dough is rounding a corner, it may need to be pleated regularly as you go forward. If an edge rips, just pinch it back together and keep going. That's the beauty of making a dessert with the word "rustic" in it!

In a small bowl, whisk the remaining egg with 1 Tbsp cold water. Brush the egg wash over the dough and sprinkle with the turbinado sugar and the remaining 1 Tbsp pistachios. Bake for 40 to 50 minutes, until the crust is deep golden brown. Transfer to a wire rack to cool. Dust with the powdered sugar. Serve warm or at room temperature.

SEASONALITY

Depending on the season, some other combos I love are almond and apple (be sure to cut your apples thinly so they cook through), hazelnut and pear, and pistachio and strawberry.

TOOL TIP

A cherry pitter is a fantastic tool that quickly punches the pits out of cherries, but if you don't cook with cherries a lot, it's not worth the money or drawer space. Instead, use a paring knife to halve the cherries and dig out the pits.

BUY SMART

Go ahead, use store-bought pie dough. Just be sure to thaw it in the refrigerator before trying to roll it out or it will crack all to pieces!

Lime Pie

My father-in-law claims to "never eat dessert," except when there's key lime pie on the menu. This rule of thumb has served him well, considering that pretty much every single restaurant on the East Coast serves key lime pie. I use normal limes in my pie because even the thought of squeezing enough of those tiny limes to make ½ cup [120 ml] of juice makes my wrist hurt. The cracker crust is crunchy and salty to balance the tart sweetness of the lime curd.

SERVES 6 TO 8

1½ sleeves Saltine crackers (about 1½ cups [210 g] pulverized)

3 Tbsp sugar

1 large egg white

½ cup (1 stick [110 g]) unsalted butter, melted

One 14-oz [420-ml] can sweetened condensed milk

½ cup [120 ml] fresh lime juice (from about 4 limes)

1 Tbsp lime zest

4 large egg yolks

1 Tbsp raspberry jam

Preheat the oven to 350°F [180°C]. Butter a 10-in [25-cm] tart pan with a removable bottom and set aside.

In a food processor or blender, combine the crackers and sugar and process until the crackers are completely crushed. Pour in the egg white and melted butter and process until combined. Transfer the mixture to the prepared tart pan and press the mixture against the sides first and then against the bottom to create a smooth crust. Place the tart pan on a baking sheet and bake for 10 minutes. Remove from the oven and cool completely.

Meanwhile, in a medium bowl, beat together the condensed milk, lime juice, lime zest, and egg yolks until combined. When the crust is cool, pour the mixture into the crust. Spoon 6 or so little dollops of raspberry jam on top and use a fork or toothpick to swirl it into the lime mixture.

Bake for 15 minutes, or until the center is no longer wobbly.

DO YOUR THING

No raspberry jam lurking in your fridge? Use whatever you have: strawberry, blueberry, cherry . . . they'll all be great! No jam at all? Just leave it out, no sweat. Make a more traditional lime pie by using 1½ cups pulverized graham crackers instead of saltines.

BUY SMART

A lot of grocery stores now sell fresh lime and lemon juice in the refrigerated section. A pie made with fresh grapefruit juice would also be delicious!

Milk Chocolate Pretzel Tart

This dessert is the pie version of a chocolate-covered pretzel: crunchy, chocolaty, and salty. As a bonus, you'll learn how to make a basic chocolate cream pie, a base you can use with any pie or tart dough.

SERVES 6 TO 8

4½ cups (about 6 oz [70 g]) hand-crushed pretzels, plus more for garnishing

1 Tbsp sugar

1 large egg white, at room temperature

1 cup (2 sticks [220 g]) unsalted butter, melted

1½ cups [360 ml] heavy cream

12 oz [340 g] milk chocolate, broken into chunks

1 large egg, at room temperature

1 tsp vanilla extract

Preheat the oven to 350°F [180°C]. Butter a 10-in [25-cm] tart pan with a removable bottom and set aside.

To make the crust: In a food processor or blender, process the pretzels and sugar until completely crushed. Drizzle in the egg white and butter and process until combined. Transfer the pretzel mixture to the prepared tart pan and press the mixture against the sides first and against the bottom to create a smooth crust. Place the tart pan on a baking sheet and bake for 10 minutes. Remove from the oven and cool completely.

To make the filling: In a medium saucepan over medium heat, heat the heavy cream to a light simmer. Remove from the heat and quickly whisk in the milk chocolate. Cool slightly, for about 3 minutes, and whisk in the egg and vanilla. Pour the filling into the (completely cooled) pretzel shell and bake for 20 minutes, or until the edges are set but the center is still wobbly.

Remove the tart from the oven, garnish with pretzel pieces, and let cool at room temperature for at least 1 hour. If you are not serving this immediately, don't add the pretzel garnish now, as they become soggy in the refrigerator.

DO YOUR THING

Instead of, or in addition to, garnishing with pretzels, you can make this tart seasonally appropriate by garnishing with crushed mini Cadbury eggs at Easter or red and green M&Ms at Christmas, or other colored candies appropriate to any holiday you're celebrating!

COOKING SCHOOL

If it seems annoying to have to wait until the tart shell is cool to pour in the filling, it is! But, it's also very important. If you don't wait until the shell cools completely, it will have a soft, soggy bite.

10-Minute Pots de Crème

When I owned my catering company in San Diego, anytime George wasn't deployed, he was forcibly employed as my sous chef (free labor!). He loved pot de crème duty because this recipe is so, so simple . . . and because he got to lick the spatula afterward.

SERVES 2

4 oz [115 g] semisweet chocolate chips

2 large eggs, at room temperature

1 tsp vanilla extract

⅛ tsp kosher salt

⅓ cup [80 ml] strong, very hot coffee

Crème fraîche and chocolate shavings for topping (optional)

In a blender, combine the chocolate chips, eggs, vanilla, and salt. Blend until coarsely blended, about 10 seconds. Turn off the motor, scrape down the sides, and pour in the (very hot!) coffee. Blend on high speed for 30 seconds to 1 minute until no specks remain and the mixture is completely smooth. Divide the chocolate mixture between two small vessels (jars or small glass cups work well), cover, and refrigerate for at least 1 hour, but up to several days before serving.

When serving, top with crème fraîche and chocolate shavings, if desired.

DO YOUR THING

This recipe easily triples for a crowd. Don't worry if you don't have six matching glass vessels; it's a fun rustic look if everyone has a different container. I also like to pour it into shot glasses and serve with demitasse spoons for a cute mini dessert.

BUY SMART

Don't waste a pot of coffee to make this: If I know I'm making this later in the day, I like to reserve ⅓ cup [80 ml] of coffee from my morning pot and heat it up for the recipe.

Bourbon Cherries with Pistachio Ice Cream

We threw a huge dinner party so all our new friends could meet my mom when she came to visit in San Diego. It turned into a real doozie of a night, and at some point in the evening, my mom started passing around mismatched coffee mugs full of ice cream topped with left-over bourbon-soaked cherries I had made for Manhattans. Everyone went *crazy* for it and still talks about that time my mom made "the best dessert ever!"

SERVES 2

½ pt [240 ml] pistachio ice cream   ¼ cup [35 g] Bourbon-Soaked Cherries (Page 119)

Divide the ice cream between two bowls. Spoon the cherries and a bit of their juice over the top.

MAKE AHEAD

When I plan to serve ice cream to a big crew, I like to pre-scoop the ice cream into individual serving vessels and put them in the freezer until it's time to serve.

DO YOUR THING

Fancy up this dessert a bit by sticking a North Carolina Wedding Cookie (page 241) into the ice cream scoop.

Bourbon Banana Pudding

Trifles are a Southern delicacy typically consisting of layered cookies or cake, pudding, fruit, and cream. Growing up, I vividly remember my mom making vanilla pudding from the packet and perfectly layering it with bananas and Nilla wafers in her gigantic trifle dish (a large clear glass cylindrical bowl) for dinner parties. I've updated her banana pudding a bit—making pudding from scratch is a bit tedious, but completely worth the end result, especially when laced with bourbon.

SERVES 4

FOR THE BANANA PUDDING

3 large egg yolks

¾ cup [150 g] packed dark brown sugar

¼ cup [35 g] cornstarch

¼ tsp kosher salt

2½ cups [600 ml] whole milk

¾ tsp vanilla extract

2½ Tbsp bourbon

¼ tsp ground cinnamon, plus more for garnishing

About ½ box Nilla wafer cookies, plus more, crushed, for garnishing

2 or 3 bananas, thinly sliced

FOR THE BOURBON WHIPPED CREAM

1 cup [240 ml] heavy cream

1 to 2 Tbsp powdered sugar

1 Tbsp bourbon

To make the banana pudding: In a medium bowl, whisk the egg yolks and ¼ cup [50 g] of the brown sugar until combined.

In a medium saucepan off the heat, whisk the remaining ½ cup [100 g] brown sugar, the cornstarch, salt, and 2 Tbsp of the milk. Place the pan over medium heat and very, very gradually whisk in the remaining 2 cups plus 6 tablespoons [570 ml] milk, dissolving the cornstarch thoroughly. When all the milk is incorporated, continue cooking, whisking frequently, for 3 to 5 minutes, or until thickened and beginning to bubble. Remove from the heat.

Temper the egg yolk mixture: Whisk about ¼ cup [60 ml] of the warm milk mixture into the egg yolk

mixture. Pour the tempered yolk mixture into the saucepan and whisk to combine. Return the saucepan to medium heat and whisk frequently for 5 to 7 minutes more, until thickened to pudding consistency. Stir in the vanilla, bourbon, and cinnamon. Cook for 1 minute more and remove the saucepan from the heat. Transfer the pudding to a bowl, cover with plastic wrap, placing it directly on the pudding surface so it does not form a skin, and refrigerate for at least 2 hours.

To assemble the pudding: Layer it (exactly how is up to you!) with the bananas and wafer cookies in either a medium, clear bowl (a trifle bowl is best) or in 4 to 6 individual ramekins, preferably clear. Start with a layer of wafers, followed by a layer of banana slices, followed by a layer of pudding. I like to build at least three layers, finishing with a thin layer of pudding. Wrap tightly with plastic wrap and refrigerate again for at least 2 hours so the wafers can absorb the pudding.

Just before you serve, make the bourbon whipped cream: In the bowl of a stand mixer with the whisk attachment, or in a large bowl with a handheld mixer, combine the heavy cream, 1 Tbsp powdered sugar, and the bourbon. Start whipping on low speed until the cream thickens slightly. Turn to high speed and whip until the cream holds stiff peaks, 1 to 2 minutes. Taste. Do you want it sweeter? Stir in another tsp of powdered sugar if so.

Top your pudding, or individual puddings, with the whipped cream, a sprinkle of crushed wafer cookies, and a dash of cinnamon. Pretend you're sitting in a rocking chair on a front porch in the middle of a humid Southern summer and ENJOY, y'all!

DO YOUR THING

Not into bourbon? Use 1½ tsp (total) vanilla extract in the banana pudding and ½ tsp vanilla extract in the whipped cream.

MAKE IT A MEAL

Serve this dessert after a meal of Shrooms 'n' Parmesan Grits (page 162) or Mom's Mac and Cheese (page 189) for a true taste of the South.

COOKING SCHOOL

In this recipe, you "temper" the eggs by whisking a bit of the hot milk into the eggs before completely pouring the eggs into the hot milk. Tempering eggs is very important, because if you just poured them straight into the hot liquid, they would turn into scrambled eggs!

California Date Shake

The last 30 minutes of the drive to Palm Springs is dotted with roadside stands selling freshly picked dates and date shakes. On a hot desert day after a long drive, they are the ideal treat—sweet, creamy, and *cold*—we look forward to our date shake the entire drive to Palm Springs! Traditional date shakes have only three ingredients—ice cream, milk, and dates—but I like to spice mine up with a bit of cinnamon and nutmeg. It has a faint eggnog-y vibe. I love serving milk shakes for dessert after a nice dinner—it's such a lighthearted, casual end to the evening. Or, add a little bourbon and keep the party going! This recipe makes two small, post-dinner shakes. If you're looking for a more filling dessert, double it.

MAKES 2 SMALL SHAKES

1 cup [240 g] vanilla ice cream

⅓ cup [80 ml] whole milk

5 Deglet dates, or 3 Medjool dates, pitted

2 to 4 ice cubes

½ tsp vanilla extract

¼ tsp ground cinnamon

Pinch of ground nutmeg, plus more for garnishing

In a blender, combine the ice cream, milk, dates, ice, vanilla, cinnamon, and nutmeg. Blend on high speed until combined. Pour into two chilled glasses and garnish with a sprinkle of nutmeg.

DO YOUR THING

Try adding 2 Tbsp of peanut butter or almond butter.

COOKING SCHOOL

Using the method as directed, you'll have little date bits in your shake. I don't mind them. If you want a smooth shake, soak the dates in boiling water for about 10 minutes, which helps them break down more easily.

Quick Cooking Reference Guide

NO-RECIPE BONE BROTH (STOCK)

I keep a huge freezer-safe container in my freezer and anytime I have meat or chicken bones or veggie scraps (carrot peels, stems, onion skins, etc.), I throw them in there. When the container gets full, throw its contents in a stockpot with a hefty pinch of salt and pepper. Add enough water to cover the ingredients by 3 in [7.5 cm], bring it to a boil, and turn the heat to low. Simmer, covered, for 3 hours. Strain through a fine-mesh sieve and freeze the stock or use it right away. This makes about 2 quarts of stock and will keep in your refrigerator for about 5 days.

TOASTED NUTS

Spread the nuts onto a baking sheet and roast at 325°F [165°C] for 8 to 15 minutes depending on the size of the nuts. Keep a close eye on them; they burn quickly! Store in an airtight container at room temperature for up to 1 month.

CRISPY BACON

Lay the bacon strips evenly in your largest (cold) non-stick skillet. Place the skillet over medium heat and cook for 4 to 6 minutes per side until crispy. Transfer to a paper towel–lined plate to drain.

HOW TO CHIFFONADE

Chiffonade is a fancy word for a very simple knife technique. To chiffonade, stack whatever you are cutting (leafy greens like de-ribbed kale and basil leaves are common) on top of each other, roll them up into a cigar shape, then use a very sharp knife to cut across the cigar roll into thin ribbons.

BASIC VINAIGRETTE FORMULA

In a medium bowl, whisk 3 Tbsp vinegar, 1 Tbsp Dijon mustard, and 1 tsp honey or maple syrup. While whisking, slowly pour in ¼ cup [60 ml] extra-virgin olive oil. Season with salt and pepper. Refrigerate in an airtight glass container for up to 1 week.

PESTO FORMULA

In a food processor or blender, combine 4 cups herbs and/or greens [weight varies], ⅓ cup nuts [weight varies], and ⅓ cup [10 g] grated Parmesan cheese. Process until finely chopped. With the processor running, slowly drizzle in ½ cup [120 ml] olive oil. Season with salt and pepper.

COOKED RICE

Measure the amount of rice you need for the recipe. Fill a large pot with four times the amount of water as rice. Salt the water and bring it to a boil over high heat. When it comes to a boil, add your rice. Cook for 30 minutes, drain, return the rice to the pot, cover the pot, and let sit for at least 10 minutes. Remove the lid, fluff the rice, and season with salt, as needed.

Menu Suggestions

GRAZING BREAKFAST FOR HOUSEGUESTS

Almond Earl Grey Lattes (page 50)

Hazelnut-Maple Granola (page 27)

Greek yogurt

Strawberry Rose Chia Jam (page 34)

Fresh fruit and hot-out-of-the-oven Cinnamon
    Roll Popovers (page 66)

BRUNCH WITH FRIENDS

Lots of coffee with Vanilla Cashew Coffee Creamer
(page 51)

English muffin breakfast sandwich buffet with:

Slow-Scrambled Eggs (page 49)

Soft-Boiled Eggs (page 48)

Crispy bacon (see Quick Cooking Reference
    Guide, page 263)

Sriracha-Maple Breakfast Meatballs (page 70)

Arugula, sliced tomatoes, lots of different cheeses, and
    Sriracha

SORRY-I-MADE-YOU-MAD BREAKFAST IN BED

Your biggest mug full of coffee

Fresh juice

Sautéed Spinach with Baked Eggs and Feta (page 58)

WEDDING SHOWER FOR YOUR BEST FRIEND

Pitchers of mimosas (use fresh-squeezed orange juice!)

Gazpacho with Charred Jalapeño Crema (page 99)
    served in tiny glasses

Sweet-and-Spicy Citrus Salad (page 64)

Creamy Corn Pasta (page 161)

North Carolina Wedding Cookies (page 241)

DINNER WHEN YOU FORGOT YOU ARE HAVING GUESTS OVER

Cold beer

Red Curry Mussels (page 150) with lots of good bread
    from the closest bakery

10-Minute Pots de Crème (page 258)

SUMMER PICNIC

Artichoke Tapenade (page 109) with baguette

Cherry Tomato Salad (page 214) with chunks of feta
    cheese instead of the fried goat cheese

Grilled Corn and Tahini Salad (page 224)

Store-bought rotisserie chicken cut into pieces

Coronado Cookies (page 240)

BACKYARD BARBECUE

Grilled squash and zucchini

Yogurt-Marinated Chicken Skewers
    with Yogurt Sauce (page 194)

Fresh tomatoes with basil and torn Burrata cheese

Berry Crumble (page 251) with vanilla ice cream

LUNCH AFTER A LONG HIKE

Really cold rosé wine

Mixed greens with Apple Cider Vinaigrette (page 91)

Gochujang Chicken Salad Sandwiches (page 106)

ANNIVERSARY DINNER

Cherry Manhattans (page 119)

Asparagus with Mustard Butter (page 219),
    without the eggs

Cast Iron T-Bone with Red Wine Sauce (page 179)

Classic Mashed Potatoes (page 180)

Rustic Cherry Pistachio Galette (page 252)

CASUAL COCKTAIL PARTY

Pitchers of Jam Cocktails (page 122)
Sweet Potato Biscuits (page 133)
Cheese plate with Brie, Manchego, and goat cheeses
    with honey and sea salt drizzled over the top
Pimiento Cheese (page 128) sandwiches on
    white bread, cut into bite-size pieces
Vietnamese Chicken Skewers (page 195)
    on mini skewers

SOUTHEAST ASIAN DINNER AFFAIR

Ice-cold Singha beer
Crunchy-Tangy Vietnamese Salad (page 83)
    without the chicken
Chicken and Bok Choy Khao Soi (page 190)
Fresh watermelon and mango for dessert

QUICKEST DINNER WHEN YOU'RE BOTH EXHAUSTED

Arugula tossed with chopped dates,
    champagne vinegar, and olive oil
Chicken Labneh Flatbreads (page 152)

BRUNCHY BABY SHOWER

Burrata with garlic confit (page 130)
DIY Sweet Potato Biscuits (page 133) bar with
    prosciutto, bacon, arugula, goat cheese,
    blue cheese
Hazelnut-Maple Granola (page 27) parfaits
Bellini bar with Prosecco and a variety of fresh fruit juices

LATE DINNER AFTER A DAY AT THE BEACH

Creamy Corn Pasta (double or triple the recipe),
    (page 161) with grilled shrimp
The juiciest heirloom tomatoes you can find,
    sliced and sprinkled with flaky sea salt,
    with Fried Goat Cheese (page 215) on top
Berry Crumble (page 251)

BIRTHDAY FIESTA

Frozen Watermelon Margaritas (page 120)
Tortilla chips with salsa
Grilled romaine lettuce drizzled with Avocado Cilantro
    Dressing (page 92) and scattered with Cotija cheese
    and Pickled Red Onions (page 82)
Chipotle Carnitas Tacos (page 206)

DINNER WHEN EVERYONE'S ON A DIET

Gin and (diet) tonics with lots of fresh lime juice
Beet Tzatziki (page 126) with carrots and
    bell pepper strips for dipping
Rainbow Veggie Bowls with Lemon Tahini Dressing
    (page 88) buffet with lots of different
    greens and grains
Fresh raspberries with Greek yogurt
    and honey for dessert

Acknowledgments

This book is for the newlyweds, awkward first-daters who decided to make a meal together, recent empty-nesters, fiftieth anniversary celebrators, and everyone in between. Cooking with your spouse, best friend, or partner—a glass of wine in one hand and a cookbook in the other—is one of the greatest joys in life. That this book will carry these recipes from my kitchen to yours, and that those recipes might become a part of you and your new family's life, overwhelms me to the point of tears.

So much goes into creating a cookbook, and one page of acknowledgments will never be enough to repay the hours in the kitchen, the wise advice, the grocery bills, the late night FaceTime therapy, or the temporary weight gain (sorry, George). I owe so much thanks to so many people:

Without the help of Margaret Cheatham Williams, Courtney Johnson (who cooked *every single recipe in this book*), Mary Pell Teden, Lexie George, Annie Culver, Capel Kane, Annie Sellers, Sarah and Tashi Gyatso, Marlea Kent, Maddy Kelley and Harrison Howey, Grace Bunn, Ann McCarthy, Sara Giedgowd, Sarah Peck, Will Chambers, and Nick Myott, we'd all be burning our cookies and under-seasoning our short ribs. Thank you for testing, re-testing, and giving completely unsolicited, but always appreciated, advice on how to make these recipes better.

Lily Wick and Nellie Morris, you two may be lousy in the kitchen, but your encouragement, love, and general absurdity helped this cookbook come to life in every way except the actual cooking.

Endless thanks to Sarah Smith for calling me at midnight in Bangkok with a lofty idea about a cookbook for newlyweds. How lucky am I that my agent is also one of my dearest friends?

To Linda Pugliese, Jeanne Lurvey, and Mariana Velasquez, thank you for making my recipes look so absurdly beautiful in these pages. You are my ultimate girl gang dream team. Sarah Billingsley, Camaren Subhiyah, Alice Chau, Tera Killip, Zaneta Jung, Christine Carswell, and the entire team at Chronicle Books, thank you for trusting me with the newlywed cookbook legacy, and for helping George and me share our love story through the recipes in this book.

This book is chock full of buttery Southern goodness thanks to my mother-in-law, Marsha Hodgin. Thank you for always having pimento cheese and sausage dip waiting on us when we come home to North Carolina, and for loving me like one of your own.

Annie Myott, my older sister, may never pick up my phone calls again after fielding so many last-minute recipe testing requests.

My mom, Francie Thompson, was a working mother of three who always found time to put supper on the table. Thank you for teaching me how to cook, how to love and appreciate food, and the importance of gathering around the dinner table.

Dad, thank you for DJ-ing the soundtrack to my life, always knowing the right song to play at the exact right moment ("Burning Down the House" by the Talking Heads, anytime Mom steps foot in the kitchen).

George, my love. Thank you for your radiant positivity, ceaseless energy, and for making me believe that I can achieve absolutely anything. Thank you for imitating a snooty food critic every single time I ask you for feedback on a recipe. Thank you for being the best puppy daddy to Hooper. Thank you for making me coffee every morning, and for making me watch the sunset every night. Life with you is simply the best.

Index